# *The National* **Literacy** *Strategy*

# Developing Early Writing

**Department for Education and Employment**

Department for Education and Employment
Sanctuary Buildings
Great Smith Street
London SW1P 3BT

ISBN 019 312 400 9

**Acknowledgement**
With thanks to the children, parents and staff of the following schools for the photographs used in this book:

Briset Primary School, London;
Conway Primary School, London;
Gallions Mount Primary School, London;
St Columb Major Community Primary School, Cornwall.

# Contents

# Part 1

# Foundation Stage – Reception

This book includes materials to help teachers and practitioners teach writing in the Reception year of the Foundation Stage. It should be used alongside the *Curriculum guidance for the Foundation Stage*, which is the core reference document for the Foundation Stage and sets out for teachers and practitioners the principles that should underpin teaching at this stage of education. The materials relate directly to the Reception year objectives in the National Literacy Strategy *Framework for teaching*.

In many schools, children enter the Reception class at different points in the year. The youngest will be just four years old. Teaching should be appropriate for the stage of development that children have reached on entering the Reception class. It should recognise what they already know and can do, and build from that.

Teachers and practitioners should plan how best to introduce children to the National Literacy Strategy in an appropriate way. Advice is given on page 27 of the *Curriculum guidance for the Foundation Stage* and in the leaflet *Guidance on the organisation of the National Literacy Strategy in Reception classes*. The guidance states that "it is important that the elements of the Literacy Hour are systematically covered in an appropriate way from the start of the Reception year," and explains that "Reception teachers may choose to cover the elements of the Literacy Hour across the day rather than in a single unit of time." It says that, "in order to ensure a smooth transition to the Literacy Hour in Year 1, [the Literacy Hour] should be in place by the end of the Reception year."

# Introduction and rationale

This book and CD-ROM contain materials to help teachers and practitioners teach writing in the Reception year of the Foundation Stage and through Key Stage 1. They emphasise the importance of shared writing and teaching from the objectives in the National Literacy Strategy *Framework for teaching* and the QCA early learning goals. Parts 1 and 3 of the book address generic issues on the teaching of writing with young children; Part 2 addresses each year group – Foundation Stage: Reception, Year 1 and Year 2 – individually.

Evidence from the evaluation of the early implementation of the National Literacy Strategy shows that, in most classrooms, while both reading and writing have been emphasised, the teaching of reading, particularly shared reading, has been more systematic and better structured. It is most likely that this has been a major factor in the substantial rise in reading scores between 1998 and 2000. Yet in writing, despite frequent opportunities, repeated encouragement and sensitive support from teachers, many children still find it difficult and make very slow progress. Although learning to write is intrinsically the greater challenge, there is much that teachers can do to improve children's progress.

**A successful writing classroom should include:**
- clear expectations, targets and regular observation and assessment of progress towards the targets;
- a stimulating writing environment with:
  - displayed and celebrated examples of children's own writing;
  - purposes and opportunities for writing linked to activities across the curriculum;
  - frequent uses of writing to communicate, eg through notes, reminders, lists, etc.;
  - frequent access to and encouragement to use writing materials at every opportunity;
  - opportunities to use writing in play activities;
- adults (not only teachers) as role models who use writing explicitly in the classroom or setting for a variety of purposes and demonstrate to children what they are doing, eg writing notes, completing registers, making lists, completing forms, writing labels, directions, captions, responding to children's work;
- a wide experience of reading as the primary source of knowledge about how written language looks and sounds;
- the systematic, regular and direct teaching of phonics;
- the direct teaching of handwriting with daily opportunity for practice;
- rich oral experience of telling, retelling and refining texts as a preparation for writing;
- regular shared writing to teach the skills of text composition directly;
- opportunities for supported, independent writing linked to, and developed from, shared writing;
- displays of word lists, notes and other formats for planning which represent 'work in progress' and serve both to remind children of previous learning and to provide scaffolds, checklists and support for independent writing.

## From speaking to writing

When children begin to write, they tend to write as they speak. Spoken language, however, is different from written language in a number of ways. These differences are related to the permanence of the written word, the need to be concise and explicit and the fact that the reader is often separated from the writer in time and space. Speakers can rely on context, intonation, facial expression, pauses, etc. to convey meaning and create effect. Writers often use more explicit grammatical structures, as well as other organisational features such as punctuation, paragraphs, headings, illustrations and diagrams to communicate ideas. The following two texts from a seven-year-old illustrate some of the differences:

**A**  Today we learnt about taste and Miss Ward put some things out on the table and we had to taste them and what we had to do is they all had numbers by them and we had to taste them and it had a different taste to them and we had to taste them and see if it was sweet, salt, and bitter and sour and I did not taste any sour.

**B**  Taste experiment
We had to taste foods which had different numbers to see if they tasted sweet, salt, bitter or sour. I thought the best taste was cheese and the worst was pickle. I did not find anything sour.

In these two examples, the intentions are similar – to explain the experiment. Text A recounts the events but backtracks and repeats. When written down, these repetitions stand out but when spoken, they make sense. The speaker joins all the thoughts together with 'and' and uses intonation, gesture and stress to keep the listener on track. Text B is more clearly a written recount. It contains far fewer clauses than A and joins them in more complex ways, that is by subordination rather than the continuous use of the conjunction 'and'. The effect is a more focused and free-standing account which can be read by any reader.

The growth of competence in writing also contributes importantly to the broader development of children's thinking. The more context-free and explicit nature of writing helps children become increasingly reflective about language. By structuring and restructuring ideas in writing, children extend their powers of imagination, learn to express increasingly complex, abstract and logical relationships, and develop the skills of reasoning and critical evaluation. This, in turn, feeds back into their powers of oral communication.

Three key features of writing are particularly important because they mark the differences between the grammar of spoken and written English:

**TEXT cohesion**

Throughout the primary years children should learn how to link sentences:

- in Reception year and at Key Stage 1, they should be able to create a coherent sequence of ideas;
- through Key Stage 2, they should learn to select from a wide range of connecting words and phrases, and to use verbs and pronouns consistently to create cohesive chronological and non-chronological texts to suit a variety of audiences and purposes.

**SENTENCE construction and punctuation**

- in Reception year and at Key Stage 1, the representation of ideas in sentences is a characteristic of written text which children need to be made aware of through reading and eventually learn to control in writing. Written sentences are differently structured from spoken utterances which can rely on gesture, intonation and stress to fill out the speaker's meaning;
- at Key Stage 2, the ability to link ideas within sentences by combining and sequencing clauses enables children to structure and connect ideas in a wide variety of ways, which create interest for readers and make children's writing more precise, varied, surprising and fit for purpose.

**WORD choice and modification**

- beginning in Reception year and through Key Stage 1, children should draw from their reading an increasingly rich vocabulary, and learn to select words and phrases that add colour and precision to their writing, refine its meaning and are appropriate to its audience and purpose;
- through Key Stage 2, children should learn how to enhance their meaning through the choice of words and through modifying nouns and verbs to add focus, variety and interest for the reader.

Some children pick up these features easily, but for many the nature of written text needs to be carefully taught. This learning comes in at least three important ways: firstly, through the experience of reading, which is the primary source of knowledge about the written word and how it 'sounds'; secondly, through oral telling and retelling of stories, explaining, instructing, recounting, etc. where they are helped to 'say it like the book' and, thirdly, through shared writing where the teacher focuses attention explicitly on writing text, demonstrating how to structure, punctuate and join sentences, choose appropriate vocabulary, and make meaning precise and explicit.

Through their reading, children begin to recognise important characteristics of a variety of written texts, often linked to style and voice. They will recognise and be able to use typical story openings: **Once there was ...**, **In a little town by the edge of ...**; ways of presenting dialogue: **he replied ...**, **said the little old man ...**. They become familiar with the way that instructions are written: **First, mix in the water ...**, and information is presented, **This is my raincoat. It keeps me dry ...**. They need to build experience and a repertoire of these written features and experiment with them in their own writing.

## Learning to write: the growth of control

A successful piece of writing is the product of these key compositional features and the transcriptional skills of spelling and handwriting. For a child of 5 or 6, it is a major achievement. The teachers and practitioners in Reception settings and Key Stage 1 classrooms are laying the building blocks for each of these elements of writing. Consider the following example:

Ben is nearly 6. He is in the second term of Year 1, and well settled in his class. He has a group writing session each week on a variety of topics including stories, ideas drawn from personal knowledge, or from shared class experiences, eg outings, cookery. He joins in the initial discussion, while his teacher writes key words on a whiteboard for children to use when they write. After the introductory discussion, the children are set to write. If Ben gets stuck on a word, he either copies it from the list provided or tries his own spelling. Sometimes he writes initial letters of words and leaves a gap for the bits he cannot spell but mostly he puts his hand up or goes to an adult to ask. He spends a lot of time waiting for help and often loses the thread of what he is trying to say. Towards the end of the session, Ben's teacher returns to the group, goes through each child's work with them, often sharing it with others. For those whose writing is not clear, she will often transcribe the text underneath, so others can read it.

His teacher has created a stimulating classroom environment with written material displayed, a well stocked book area and lots of story telling and book sharing with adults. Ben also practises handwriting with the teaching assistant. He has other opportunities to write through role-play and, in relation to other classroom activities, he writes lists, instructions, captions and records incidents.

Looking back over his work for the year, his teacher observes:

*Ben works hard at writing but finds it a struggle. He has done quite a lot of writing and, though there are signs of improvement, his progress has been very slow and there is a lot of unfinished work in his books. Although his handwriting is more decipherable, his spelling, even of very simple words, is still very idiosyncratic, and often difficult for him or others to read back. He writes so slowly that he often loses track of what he is trying to say. This affects the flow of his thinking and his motivation to write. I sometimes re-write the text underneath so Ben can see and read the 'correct' version but this does not seem to have had much impact on the development of his work over the year. He is still very dependent on adult help.*

Ben writes very slowly and is already becoming reluctant to write. Closer inspection of his writing experience is revealing. Despite support and encouragement from his teacher, most of his writing experience consists of working independently with very little explicit teaching about strategies for composing writing or for helping him to see his ideas through. Like Ben, many children find independent writing a struggle because they are faced with too many hard things to do at once. He has to plan what he will write, think of which words to choose and how to order them into sentences, work out the spellings for each and transcribe them all on to the page. For experienced writers, much of this is automatic, and only occasionally requires conscious control.

There are parallels with other complex skills. Experienced drivers do not need to think about the controls, which simply become an extension of themselves, leaving them free to concentrate on where they are going. The learner driver often needs someone else to take care of the pedals, so she or he can concentrate on the steering, and vice versa. This is Ben's problem: he needs to be taught to manage and co-ordinate the different writing controls in the service of concentrating on what he is writing about.

The 'searchlights' model in the National Literacy Strategy *Framework for teaching* provides a useful metaphor. Successful readers need to orchestrate a range of cues (phonic, graphic, grammatical and information drawn from the wider context of the text, its organisation and meaning). But while a reader has to decode, understand and interpret a text, a writer must invent it. For the writer, the 'searchlights' represent a range of decisions, rather than cues, that have to be orchestrated to create a text. Children need to be taught how to control and co-ordinate two key aspects of writing, as they move towards independence:

| Choices for writers | Searchlights | NLS *Framework* strands |
| --- | --- | --- |
| **Composition:** <br> ● Planning: What am I writing about and who is it for? ie content, purpose and audience <br> ● Composing: How do I say it in writing? ie word choice, sentence grammar and text organisation | Context and grammar | Text and sentence |
| **Transcription:** <br> ● How do I write it down? ie spelling and handwriting | Phonic and graphic knowledge | Word |

To make progress in writing Ben needs specific help to improve his **transcriptional skills** but he also needs to have more explicit **teaching of writing** in which the processes of composition are modelled and his writing tasks are suitably scaffolded so that he does not have to pay attention to all elements of writing all of the time.

## Transcription: teaching spelling and handwriting

These materials focus mainly on shared writing and the teaching of compositional skills, for two reasons. Firstly, there is other detailed, practical guidance on teaching phonics and spelling to which teachers should refer.[1] Secondly, the process of composing writing is often obstructed by the amount of effort required to transcribe. This can create a cycle of difficulties for children. They tend to write only the words they can confidently spell, pay too little attention to the way words and sentences go together in written language, fail to develop sense and purpose in their writing, become over-dependent on adult help and increasingly reluctant to write.

Four important points about teaching transcriptional skills should be noted, however:

● In Reception and throughout Key Stage 1, children should be taught transcriptional skills systematically and directly to develop accuracy and speed to an automatic level. These skills cannot be reliably taught as they arise 'in context', through shared writing, because they occur too randomly and infrequently. However, they should be continually and systematically *applied* in real writing contexts to secure the skills and to teach children how to draw upon and transfer their knowledge effectively.

1 The NLS *Progression in phonics* provides very clear guidance on how to teach early spelling skills in active and engaging ways. The NLS *Spelling Bank* builds on this early learning by focusing on important spelling conventions and rules. Section 3 in Part 3 of this book sets out further guidance on teaching handwriting.

- There is an important tradition of promoting developmental or emergent writing in early childhood which emphasises the value of experimentation with writing. Children benefit from opportunities to experiment and to write spontaneously, but handwriting and spelling involve conventions which are arbitrary and, therefore, not easily discoverable. For this reason, spelling and handwriting should be taught and practised directly and systematically, so that children learn the correct conventions. *Progression in phonics* contains a clear programme of teaching phonics. All YR and Key Stage 1 teachers are entitled to their own copy of this book.
- Transcriptional skills need to be practised and 'over-learned' to a point where they become habitual – and correct! In order to secure this, teaching should be little and often – at least 15 minutes per day.
- Teaching transcriptional skills can and should be active, enjoyable and successful. They can be taught to the whole class at an accelerated rate through activities which help teachers assess as they teach and differentiate to support individual pupils. Pages 156–69 contain guidance for teaching transcriptional skills.

In the early stage, teaching the skills of composition and transcription should have equal weight. As children become more skilled at the transcriptional level, the process of composition should become the dominant challenge. Teaching through shared writing is the key to this development.

# The teaching of writing

## Shared writing

Shared writing is a powerful teaching strategy and the principal means of teaching writing. It is much more than merely scribing for pupils, writing down their ideas like an enthusiastic secretary. It has an essential place in literacy teaching because it enables teachers to:

- work with the whole class, to model, explore and discuss the choices writers make at the point of writing, rather than by correction, demonstrating and sharing the compositional process directly;
- make the links between reading and writing explicit by reading and investigating how writers have used language to achieve particular effects and by using written texts as models for writing;
- scaffold some aspects of writing, eg the spelling and transcribing, to enable children to concentrate on how to compose their writing, eg through the choice of words or phrases and ways of constructing sentences to achieve particular purposes or effects;
- focus on particular aspects of the writing process, while supporting others:
  - planning
  - drafting
  - revising;
- introduce children to appropriate concepts and technical language as a means of discussing what writers do and internalising principles to apply to their own writing;
- provide an essential step towards independent writing by helping children to understand and apply specific skills and strategies.

### Key features of shared writing

During shared writing it is important for the teacher or practitioner to:

- identify **specific text and sentence level** objectives from the National Literacy Strategy *Framework*;
- discuss the content and purpose of the writing, telling and retelling to get ideas clear, reveal the overall structure and begin to frame it in 'writerly' language;
- capture and organise ideas in a **writing plan**;
- **rehearse sentences orally** before writing them down;
- **constantly and cumulatively reread** to gain a flow from one sentence into another – as well as checking for possible improvements or errors;
- encourage the **automatic** use of basic punctuation;
- **discuss and explain** why one decision might be preferable to another;
- pause during the writing to focus discussion upon the specific objective, but otherwise, move the rest of the composition on quickly so that the children's attention is not lost;
- take suggestions from children who will make effective contributions but also ask children who may struggle, in order **to check misconceptions** and provide further opportunities for explanation. These children should be specifically checked on when they are using dry-wipe boards to assure the quality of their writing. Where some children remain uncertain, they may be targeted as a guided group;
- make the occasional **deliberate error** to hold children's attention and focus on common errors or an error related to the specific objective being taught.

Writing, even at the simplest level, demands reflection on, and restructuring of, ideas in a relatively abstract form. For most young writers, this process needs a lot of support. The materials that follow are built around the following sequence, designed to scaffold the process, enabling children to concentrate on certain aspects of writing without having to deal with all the others simultaneously, and to work effectively towards independent writing:

---

### 1 Planning writing

- *Talk for writing*: discussion to clarify the content and purpose of the writing, telling and retelling to get ideas clear, reveal the overall structure and begin to frame it in 'writerly' language
- *Making a plan*: recording the intended text in note, picture or diagrammatic form from which to compose the text in shared and independent writing

### 2 Shared writing

- *Teacher demonstration*: working from the 'talk for writing' to show how a text is written
- *Teacher scribing*: to write for the children while they compose and contribute all or some of the text
- *Supported composition*: occasions in the course of shared writing when children write parts of the text, possibly in pairs, eg on dry-wipe boards

### 3 Independent but supported writing

Independent writing at an appropriate level to complete, insert into, extend, modify, etc. work started in the shared task

---

## Planning writing

TALK FOR WRITING

Too often, children are expected to write without being clear about *what* they are trying to say. Writing should start from talking – discussion which helps to capture content and purpose. This needs to go well beyond simply providing stimulating ideas and should help children to capture the content, sequence and style of what they are about to write. Children should know, and have rehearsed, what they are trying to write and not be left to make it up as they go along. This immediately provides a lot of support.

- It helps children to keep the 'story' in their heads, giving them a clear sense of the overall text, particularly how it should end.
- It guides how the text should sound – its style and voice.
- It helps children to sequence and structure their writing, to know where it is going and how it should be joined together to make sense.
- It provides the crucial point of reference against which to check for sense: 'If I know what I am trying to say, I can tell if it is clear and sensible. If I am making it up as I go along, how do I know if I am going in the right direction?'

Talk for writing should be used to:

- recall or invent the content of what is to be written so that the whole sequence is clear. It might be a retold story, an anecdote from personal experience, a recount of a class activity, captions to provide information, an instruction, a letter, a note, an invitation, an enquiry, etc. The content and structure should be made explicit. This might be done through discussion, role-play or the use of puppets. It should also draw extensively on work from other subjects where this discussion and the capturing of it in a writing plan may be done at other times, eg as part of a cooking activity, a class visit, a science observation, a constructional activity;
- generate and rehearse appropriate language, giving special attention to the ways in which written language differs from speech.

MAKING A WRITING PLAN

It is often helpful to capture the outline and structure of the discussion in a concrete plan for writing. You can draw this together in the course of discussion. As well as creating a writing plan, it helps you model a variety of ways of representing ideas. For example, you might create:

- sequences of pictures or diagrams to show the events in a story or a process;
- story maps to show how a story moves from time to time and place to place;
- timelines to show a series of events for a recounted experience;
- a picture of one or more characters with labelling;
- relationship maps;
- setting or character using objects, models, puppets, etc.;
- a writing frame;
- a list of notes and reminders.

Planning is an investment in subsequent control – don't be afraid to give it time. Make the process explicit and help children to do it for themselves. Older and more able Key Stage 1 children who have some experience of planning for writing should be encouraged to work out their own writing plans. This can become a task for group and independent work for use in subsequent Literacy Hours.

## Shared writing

Use shared writing to teach children how to translate the writing plan (or writing intentions, if they are not recorded) into a written text. The plan is a helpful bridge between thinking and writing. Focus attention on how written language sounds and is structured in order to:

- transform speech into sentences;
- select appropriate vocabulary: words and phrases;
- choose from a range of connectives to sequence and structure the text;
- use style and voice appropriate to the type of text, its purpose and audience.

TEACHER DEMONSTRATION

Most shared writing sessions begin with demonstration by the teacher or practitioner, modelling how the text is composed – maintaining a clear focus on the objective(s). The teacher thinks the process through aloud, rehearsing the sentence before writing, making changes to its construction or word choice and explaining why one form or word is preferable to another. She or he writes the sentence, rereads it and changes it again if necessary, and then demonstrates at least two sentences. The children's role is to listen carefully as they will soon attempt writing a similar text or using a similar feature themselves. Every so often shared writing is used to orchestrate a number of different objectives, calling upon all that has been learned so far.

TEACHER SCRIBING (WHOLE CLASS COMPOSITION)

The children now make contributions building upon the teacher's initial demonstration. The teacher focuses and limits the children's contributions to the objective(s), eg previous sentence level work, reading of similar texts, word level work, prompt sheets, writing frameworks or planning sheets. The teacher challenges children's contributions in order to refine their understanding and compositional skills.

The teacher might ask the children to discuss their contributions with one another before offering them for inclusion in the class composition. The children can offer their contributions by raising their hands, but with older children more considered contributions and fuller class

participation can be achieved by asking the children, individually or in pairs, to note down their idea. When the teacher receives a contribution from the children, she or he will explain its merits or ask the children to do so. The teacher may ask for a number of contributions before making and explaining her or his choice. If the children use dry-wipe boards and thick-nibbed pens, they can hold up their contributions for the teacher to read. The teacher can then decide either to choose a contribution that will move the lesson on quickly or a contribution which will stimulate discussion and offer the opportunity to make a teaching point.

SUPPORTED COMPOSITION
The focus here is on the children's composition. Children may use dry-wipe boards or notebooks to write in pairs, or individually, a limited amount of text, sharply focused upon a specific objective. This needs to be swift, and once sentences are completed they should be held up so that the teacher can make an immediate assessment. Successful examples can be reviewed with the class, whilst misconceptions are identified and corrected.

In Year 2, from time to time, supported composition should be allowed longer than 15 minutes in order to orchestrate recent work on language effects, sentence construction or organisation of a particular text type. How to plan using a range of different strategies, how to translate a plan into a fluent first draft, how to revise for improvements and how to check for errors will all be considered in different 15-minute shared writing sessions over the year. However, it is essential to bring these elements together to serve a specific composition in which the writer is also required to consider effective use of language and sentence construction in a supported context.

During an extended supported composition period of 50 minutes (using the 30-minute whole class teaching time and the 20-minute independent working time), the teacher directs the organisation of the composition in two or three mid-plenaries and the children construct their own text individually or in pairs.

## Independent writing

Guided writing cannot always be used as a stepping stone into independent writing and, for many children, the move from shared to independent writing should be manageable. Nevertheless, to achieve this, the shared writing needs to be carefully planned to provide the kind of support most likely to help children towards independence. The points above on:

- talking for writing;
- writing plans;
- teacher demonstration;
- teacher scribing;
- supported composition;

have been made with this in mind and you should plan to move through this sequence as a preparation for independent writing. The focus of the work in shared writing should be continued into purposeful writing tasks through which children apply their new learning. Shared writing sessions can be used to scaffold independent writing in a number of ways, for example by providing:

- a variation on a well-known story;
- a worked out writing plan for children to write to. This might be a story but could be a non-fiction plan linked to one of the text types and related to work in other subjects;
- a partially worked text for children to complete or 'infill';
- the beginning of a poem in which each line starts the same way;
- outlines of a story plot using, eg captions, pictures, arrows, to indicate main incidents in order;
- a bank of relevant vocabulary: words and phrases;
- an outline in note form or as a flow chart for children to expand in full sentences;
- a diagram for which instructions can be added;
- a poem, to substitute new lines;
- questions to form the plan, eg an evaluation of a book.

Using this general pattern of support, teachers can plan to move children to increasing autonomy in their writing. As they become more familiar and successful in these relatively scaffolded, independent tasks, the props can be removed. You must judge the rate and sequence of this process. Certainly, children should always have plenty of opportunity in all aspects of their work to write independently and we must be careful not to allow the structure of teaching through shared writing to slow children down or lower expectations.

Model writing behaviours in shared writing which children will emulate when they write independently. Articulate these behaviours in the form of prompts to yourself, eg *'Do I know what I want to write? Tell it to myself. Make a writing plan so I can remember the important points. Rehearse each sentence carefully before I write it down. Reread as I write to keep the flow and make sure it makes sense.'* Modelling what to do when you 'get stuck' is also very helpful. Not only is it reassuring to children to know that 'getting stuck' is a normal condition, it gives them strategies for moving on.

**If I get stuck**

- Go back to my writing plan to remind myself of the big picture.
- Think about who and what the writing is for, and talk it through.
- Reread what I have written to get the sense and flow of what comes next.
- Rehearse aloud or in my head the whole sentence I am trying to write.
- Think ahead to what is supposed to come next or how the writing should end.
- If I am stuck on a word:
  - find another one that will do for now and come back to this one later or even leave a gap;
  - refer to spelling strategies – three things I should do before asking an adult.

THE PLACE OF GUIDED WRITING

In most classes, the arithmetic of time means that children will spend substantially less time being taught in groups than in the whole class. The priority for group work in literacy in Reception and at Key Stage 1 should be given to the teaching of reading. This is partly because of the nature of reading which must be heard to be effectively taught, but also because, as indicated in the teaching sequence set out above, most children can move from shared to independent work without the need for group work, provided the shift is carefully managed. Of course, guided writing time in groups has important and obvious advantages over working with a whole class but, because it is in relatively short supply in most classes, you need to target it wisely. Much of the guidance on shared writing above applies equally to guided writing. The main difference is that guided writing, like guided reading, can provide an additional supported step towards independent writing, where the onus is on the children to make decisions, compose and revise their own texts. Guided writing should be planned with three major purposes in mind:

- to support children in planning and drafting their own work;
- to revise and edit and evaluate work in progress;
- to provide differentiated support for particular groups:
  - to rerun a shared writing session with more support and focus for less secure writers;
  - to prepare a group of children who are learning English as an additional language in advance of a shared writing session;
  - to work intensively with able writers on composing or editing a draft;
  - to work intensively on supported independent writing with less able writers.

## Planning for teaching of writing in the Literacy Hour

The National Literacy Strategy *Framework for teaching* gives some guidance on the balance of time to be spent on teaching the various aspects of literacy. Since it was written, some teachers have found that there are several different ways of rearranging the component parts of the Literacy Hour. Many have found that teaching the word level work at the start of the lesson has been helpful. In other classes, teachers plan for separate or additional phonics sessions or additional guided reading and writing sessions for particular groups.

The summary below offers a guide to the balance of time for class work in each year at Key Stage 1 with a view to securing time for the teaching of writing. It is not a rigid prescription but should be used as a baseline for evaluating variations against the need to maintain the overall balance of teaching across the week.

## GUIDE TO BALANCE OF WHOLE CLASS WORK

| Y1 | | | |
|---|---|---|---|
| 5 days per fortnight | | 5 days per fortnight | |
| Phonics/spelling | 15 minutes per day | Phonics/spelling | 15 minutes per day |
| Shared reading | 15 minutes per day | Shared writing | 15 minutes per day |

## GUIDE TO BALANCE OF WHOLE CLASS WORK

| Y2 | | | |
|---|---|---|---|
| 5 days per fortnight | | 5 days per fortnight | |
| Phonics/spelling | 15 minutes per day | Shared writing to cover sentence and text level objectives | 30 minutes per day |
| Shared reading | 15 minutes per day | | |

### PRINCIPLES

- In Year 1, phonics (and sometimes other spelling) should be taught every day for at least 15 minutes. This could take place at the beginning of the Literacy Hour or at any time of day, possibly in two shorter sessions. In a mixed age class, two different phonics sessions may need to be taught daily to cater for children at different levels.
- In Year 2, sentence level work should be the specific teaching focus for two days a week drawing on high quality written texts but integral to the teaching of shared writing.
- In Year 2, it may occasionally be appropriate to treat the first 30 minutes of the Literacy Hour as a continuous teaching sequence with focused attention on particular grammatical features as an integral part. In the course of this time, children should:
  - work from examples of written texts, to explore how grammatical features are used to create particular effects;
  - investigate these features through activities such as cloze, transforming sentences, collecting and classifying words and phrases to understand principles and conventions;
  - apply this knowledge in composing texts through shared writing.

  This sequence may be planned over several days for continuity and extension work and to develop shared writing into independent writing.

## Targets and assessment

These materials have also been designed to help teachers identify and set clear writing targets. Children's confidence in writing will grow from aiming for and achieving success. In the introduction to each block of teaching units are annual target statements for writing. These statements summarise the objectives from the National Literacy Strategy *Framework for teaching* into a set of end-of-year expectations for children in each year group. At Reception, these target statements are aligned with the early learning goals. Targets are useful for explaining to children what they are expected to learn about writing and to involve them in evaluating their own progress. For most children, group targets or whole class targets will suffice. These may then be adjusted to suit individual needs with more specific individual targets, where necessary.

Targets can be phrased effectively in the form of *'I can …'* statements. Teachers and practitioners can use these statements as a focus for class discussion, particularly in plenary sessions, and for marking children's work. Such statements enable children to gain control, aim for specific improvements in their own work and, above all, earn praise, encouragement and recognition for success. Targets also provide a focus for discussion with parents and for records of achievement as the child moves through the term and the year. Examples of such statements might include: *'I can write a list.'* (Reception); *'I can use a capital letter and full stop to punctuate a sentence.'* (Year 1); *'I can write in a range of forms and know who I am writing for and why.'* (Year 2).

## How to use these materials

Part 2 of these materials contains units of work for teaching writing. These units:

- are driven by **text** level objectives;
- incorporate **sentence** level objectives;
- apply **word** level objectives.

The units exemplify how to teach the writing objectives in the National Literacy Strategy *Framework for teaching*. They do not attempt to cover all the text level objectives as this would remove the choice of text from the teacher and restrict flexibility in the class timetable for the other curriculum areas in which writing occurs. In each year there is additional material to show how further sentence level objectives may be covered. The teaching units could be reused with different subject matter (curriculum area/text) or could act as models for incorporating sentence level objectives with other text level objectives.

The units state a writing target and expected outcome and usually cover two or more text level objectives and a number of sentence and word level objectives. Each unit opens by setting the context of what work has to be covered prior to the unit such as learning about a text type in shared reading and/or an activity in another curriculum area such as a visit, a construction or an experiment. Most teaching units contain several writing sessions. These usually open with 'Talk for writing' and move into one or more forms of shared writing. Suggestions for independent activities and the plenary are provided. There are also suggestions for the next teaching step.

Part 3 of these materials contains useful reference material on text features and the transcriptional skills of handwriting and spelling.

## CD-ROM

The CD-ROM in the inside cover of this book contains:

- revised glossary, also on the DfEE Standards website: http://www.standards.dfee.gov.uk/literacy/glossary/;
- target statements for writing;
- text and materials for Year 2 sentence level units on pages 122–49.

# Part 2
## The teaching units

# Foundation Stage: Reception year

## Contents

**Reception year units:**

|  | Objectives | | Early learning goals | Page |
|---|---|---|---|---|
| **Unit 1:**<br>**The Supermarket** | **T1a** | to recognise printed and handwritten words in a variety of settings …; | • Enjoy listening to and using spoken and written language …<br>• Extend their vocabulary …<br>• Use language to imagine and recreate roles and experiences<br>• Use talk to organise, sequence and clarify thinking, ideas, feelings and events<br>• Use their phonic knowledge to write simple regular words …<br>• Attempt writing for different purposes … | 32 |
|  | **T1b** | that words can be written down again for a wide range of purposes; | | |
|  | **T11a** | to understand that writing can be used for a range of purposes | | |
|  | **T11b** | to understand that writing remains constant …; | | |
| **Unit 2:**<br>**The Bear Hunt** | **T7** | to use knowledge of familiar texts to re-enact or re-tell to others, recounting the main points in correct sequence; | • Extend their vocabulary …<br>• Use language to imagine and recreate roles and experiences<br>• Use talk to organise, sequence and clarify thinking, ideas, feelings and events<br>• Explore and experiment with sounds, words and texts<br>• Retell narratives in the correct sequence …with adults;<br>• Use their phonic knowledge to write simple regular words …<br>• Attempt writing for different purposes …<br>• Write their own names … begin to form simple sentences | 37 |
|  | **T14** | to use experience of stories, poems and simple recounts as a basis for independent writing … and through shared composition with adults | | |
|  | **S1** | to expect written text to make sense and check for sense if it does not; | | |
| **Unit 3:**<br>**The Exhibition** | **T12** | to write labels or captions for pictures and drawings; | • Write their own names … begin to form simple sentences …<br>• Extend their vocabulary … | 43 |
|  | **S1** | to expect written text to make sense and check for sense if it does not; | | |
|  | **W6** | to read on sight the 45 high frequency words to be taught by the end of YR, from Appendix List 1; | | |

# Introduction

The early learning goals for communication, language and literacy[1] outline what most children will be able to achieve in writing by the end of the Foundation Stage. The *Curriculum guidance for the Foundation Stage* contains detailed guidance for teachers and practitioners to support children in learning to write (page 44 'Communication, language and literacy'). However, all the areas of learning as defined in the guidance contribute to children's developing ability to write. Some contribute more to the content of the writing, eg 'Knowledge and understanding of the world' and some more to the physical aspect of handwriting, eg 'Physical development', but there are aspects in all areas which influence the process of learning to write.

Likewise, within the area 'Communication, language and literacy', all the elements have a direct bearing on writing and the specific pages on which each is covered in the *Curriculum guidance for the Foundation Stage* are indicated below. Young children learn how to write through:

- developing oral language  (pages 48–59);
- reading with an adult individually and/or in a group (pages 62–3);
- playing games which help them to hear sounds in words and form the letters that represent them (early spelling and handwriting) (pages 60–1 and 66–7);
- playing and experimenting with writing (pages 64–5) and watching others write (shared writing).

## The role of oral language and reading in developing writing
Much of what children need to learn about writing, from story-structure to written language features and punctuation, can be gained from story telling, shared reading, and the oral interaction stimulated by them.

1 *Curriculum guidance for the Foundation Stage* (QCA/DfEE 2000), ref. QCA/00/587

- Retell tales yourself, especially favourites, and give opportunities for the children to join in.
- Identify the main incidents – illustrate them if possible, to make a class book or wall display.
- Encourage the children to retell stories and recount their own experiences.
- Encourage re-enacting in drama, dressing up, converting the role-play area into a bears' cave, a supermarket, and so on. These situations provide opportunities for children to use and re-use new sentence structures and become familiar with the language of stories.
- Discuss characters' actions and reactions when you read to children, consider the consequences of their actions, and look at how stories are built up and concluded.
- Introduce children to a range of printed and handwritten texts in a variety of situations, eg stories, poems, rhymes, notes, registers, labels, signs, notices, letters, forms, lists, directions, advertisements, newspapers.
- Make active use of the print displayed in the classroom, around the setting and in the local area, eg by discussing relevant notices around the sink when washing up, or taking children on 'print walks' and encouraging talk and discussion about the messages conveyed.
- Mimic the literary effects such as **Once upon a time … , and he walked on and on until … , There was once a … .**
- Take opportunities to draw children's attention to English print conventions such as directionality and use correct terms so that children begin to use them for themselves, eg **book**, **cover**, **beginning**, **end**, **page**, **words**, **letter**, **title**, **sentence**.
- Draw the children's attention to words and sentences and ask them to show you 'a word' and to draw their fingers along a sentence from capital letter to full stop.

## Spelling and handwriting

Playing games every day to help children to hear sounds in words and recognise the letters that correspond to the sounds will greatly advance children's ability and confidence to write. Very quickly, they begin to write recognisable words and are then able to read their own writing. The National Literacy Strategy publication *Progression in phonics* is designed for this purpose. It provides a programme of activities which can be carried out with large or small groups of children. The importance of this element of writing cannot be over-emphasised. Section 4 in Part 3 of this book summarises the approach taken in *Progression in phonics*.

In the Reception year, children will wish to write some common *irregular* key words, eg **was**, **the**, **said**, and these should be taught as whole words rather than by the phonemic strategy (see the Reception list in the Appendix to the National Literacy Strategy *Framework for teaching*). There are many common words in this list to which the phonic strategy can be applied, eg **on**, **this**, **yes**.

Similarly, it is crucial to lay the foundation for pencil control and correctly formed letters. Activities for developing gross and fine motor control and the movements involved in the formation of the letters of the alphabet are contained in Section 3 in Part 3 of this book.

## Independent writing, playing and experimenting

The teacher or practitioner is a major influence in developing children as writers so that their competence and control develops with enjoyment. It is essential that you create an environment which actively cultivates, promotes and encourages children to write.

● Provide purposeful and real experiences across the six areas of the Foundation curriculum, eg play scenarios using props which encourage writing, such as notepads at the telephone for messages, appointment card at the hairdressers, or cheque books at the bank. The home corner could have magnetic letters on the fridge door, calendars to mark the date, telephone message pads, a desk containing material for writing letters, stamps, bills, cheque books, etc.

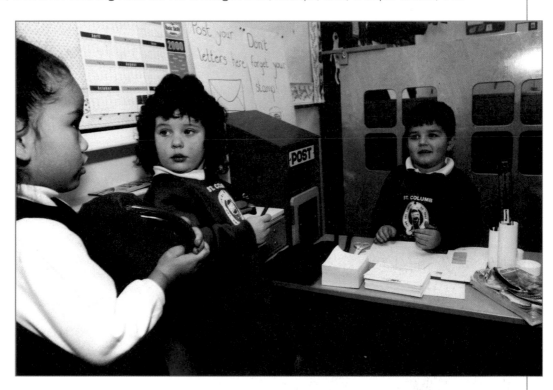

● Share and celebrate examples of children's writing, eg shopping lists, birthday cards.
● Provide frequent opportunities for writing to communicate, eg through notes, reminders, lists, and access to and encouragement to use writing materials in meaningful situations.
● Involve the children in creating and modifying interactive wall displays containing print.
● Provide a warm, light and comfortable book area.
● Ensure a variety of play scenarios which help children to develop fine motor skills for effective pencil control.
● Provide a rich oral experience of telling and retelling stories as a preparation for writing.
● Display notices, instructions and directions which help children, their families and carers to find their way about and make sense of the environment, and which both remind children of previous learning and provide scaffolds, support and resources for independent writing.

Children in the Foundation Stage often use emergent writing long before they can read. They do so spontaneously, and with concentration, pleasure and interest if they are free to experiment and are encouraged to ask questions about print and writing. Children will draw and paint, giving meaning to the marks they make, and begin to try out writing as a means of recording and communicating. They will often use the letters in their own name in their early attempts to use conventional writing in English. Eventually, as they begin to discriminate the phonemes in words, they use the letters they know to represent them.

The role-play area and writing corner provide opportunities for children to use their developing skills and knowledge to experiment. Often this will be initiated by the child and can be enhanced if you or other adults model writing in the role-play area – for instance, writing envelopes in a post office or the bill in a restaurant.

Seize on any purposeful opportunity to write. In the same way that talk develops because we need to communicate, and reading develops because we like to read, writing develops when we see the point of it – a purpose and an audience are crucial. Children need to experience writing in different contexts – stories to entertain, messages to inform, lists to help organise, greetings cards, directions, signs, letters to invite parents and friends to a party, messages sent to a storytime character, information written to help another class, labels put up to inform people about a display, etc. Captions, for instance, provide an early form of sentence making that has a clear purpose for young writers.

Children, like all of us, write best about what they know. For this reason, writing recounts about significant events is important. As they become familiar with non-fiction, poems and stories, these too can become a basis for their own writing – retelling, substituting, extending.

It is important to value children's earliest attempts at writing and recognise them as steps along the route to writing fluently. Ask children to reread what they have written, to add an illustration or pin their writing to a noticeboard. In this way, children begin to gain a sense that writing is something that they can do. At the same time, note significant developmental stages, such as writing from left to right, top to bottom, beginning to leave a space between words, investing their own words with meaning.

Respond to children's writing as a reader. Comment upon its success as communication, before you comment on specific aspects of transcription. Celebrate new developments (longer sentences, use of an adjective, use of initial and end sound, etc.). Write messages and responses back to the child, eg 'John, It sounds like a great weekend.'

If you write the conventional version of a sentence beneath a child's version, praise the places where the child has been able to match spelling – perhaps an initial letter – or to separate words. This helps the child gain a sense of how their writing is beginning to move towards the sorts of conventions they notice in their word level work and reading.

Adult scribing, or the use of audio tapes, helps to encourage extended composition. This can be enlightening, as children's ability to compose may well outstrip their secretarial skills by a long way. Some of the children's own compositions can be usefully turned into short booklets for their own reading material, display or the book area.

It is established good practice for adults to consider and build upon the different starting points from which children will develop their concepts of print. Previous experiences will be wide ranging, and in the case of children who are learning English as an additional language may include experiences of a print system where the rules differ from those of English. Experience of other language systems needs to be acknowledged and valued and the differences explored in discussion with the children.

## Using shared writing in the Reception year

As described in Part 1 of this book, shared writing is a powerful medium for demonstrating and developing the compositional aspects of writing and this is the focus of the three units for Reception year in this book. However, throughout the Foundation Stage, shared writing – making the process of writing visible and explicit – can develop children's understanding of print. A book is an object, a finished product of writing; children do not at first associate books with the *process* of writing.

- Make daily opportunities to use writing to communicate with others, to record events or provide reminders of future events, to label classroom equipment, to show where to find things or to identify them for use at a particular time or by particular children.

- Create purposes for making lists and for writing notices and find reasons to keep replacing the classroom print so that you get plenty of opportunity to write in front of the children. When children see the purpose and the usefulness of writing they are very likely to opt to write when given opportunities.

- Draw children's attention to the place on the whiteboard or flip chart where you start to write and comment on the movement from left to write and top to bottom. This is particularly important when there are children who are also learning other writing systems with different directionality. The *Curriculum guidance for the Foundation Stage* has a very important section on the value of linguistic diversity (page 19).

- Say the words aloud as you write them. This helps the children to realise that the speech stream is composed of units (words), some of which take up more space than others on the page but which have a similar sized gap between them.

- Encourage the idea of spaces between words by rehearsing sentences before writing them and counting the number of words in the sentence after writing. Spaces may well then appear in the children's own writing, even though the words they use are not necessarily conventionally spelled.

- Establish quite early the use of capital initial letters for people's names. Children like to label their own work with their names, and often make the breakthrough to phonemic awareness through hearing and knowing the first sound in their own name. Later you can extend the 'naming' of work to the writing of simple captions or labels for drawings, etc.

- Demonstrate, as you write, how to segment words into sounds and blend them back to words. Ask children to listen to a word, say it slowly and listen for the sounds. To start with they will probably be able to contribute only the initial sound. Soon they will also be able to identify the final sound, and later the medial sound.

  They could have a go at this using individual dry-wipe boards; this is more inclusive than one child going to write on the class whiteboard. Eventually they should be able to spell many of the simple consonant-vowel-consonant (CVC) words you use in writing, but be sparing with spelling contributions from children in shared writing; the object is for them to recognise how to apply their spelling knowledge, not to turn shared writing into a phonics lesson. The *Progression in phonics* games will do the same job much more quickly. So, only pick out occasional words for them to 'help' you with.

The National Literacy Strategy *Framework for teaching* objectives for writing are in line with the early learning goals which most children will achieve at the end of the Foundation Stage Reception year. The three units of work for teaching writing in the Reception year are based on the teaching sequence outlined in Part 1 of this book. 'Talk for writing' is an essential element of the sequence and the content for this is clearly outlined in each session of the units. The units are designed to be taught over a number of different sessions, possibly over a fortnight. In each unit the children will be working towards early learning goals from NLS objectives. These units are examples of the sort of activities through which teachers and practitioners engage children in order to develop their writing. They do not exemplify all the text level objectives but do offer an example of different text types.

The National Literacy Strategy target statements for writing at the end of the Reception year break down the compositional aspect of writing contained in the early learning goals. By the end of the Foundation Stage, in writing, most children will be able to:

| Early learning goals | | Target statements for writing |
|---|---|---|
| • Use their phonic knowledge to write simple regular words and make phonetically plausible attempts at more complex words. | Phonics and spelling | • Spell CVC words, eg **shop**, **leg**, **rich**.<br>• Attempt to spell unfamiliar words using a phonemic strategy (including analogy).<br>• Spell some words for YR in Appendix List 1 in the NLS *Framework*. |
| • Use a pencil and hold it effectively to form recognisable letters, most of which are correctly formed. | Handwriting | • Write letters using the correct sequence of movements. |
| • Extend their vocabulary, exploring the meaning and sounds of new words. | Style: language effects | • Begin to use some story language, such as **Once upon a time…** . |
| • Write their own names and other things such as labels and captions and begin to form sentences, sometimes using punctuation. | Style: sentence construction | • Dictate a simple sentence.<br>• Begin to write simple sentences. |
| | Punctuation | • Write own name, using a capital letter.<br>• Begin to use capital letters and full stops to punctuate a sentence. |
| • Attempt writing for various purposes, using features of different forms such as lists, stories and instructions. | Purpose and organisation | • Retell a narrative or a recount.<br>• Begin to write simple narratives and recounts.<br>• Invest writing with meaning. Write simple labels, captions and sentences. |
| • Retell narratives in the correct sequence, drawing on the language patterns of stories. | Process | • Dictate and invent own compositions.<br>• Think about what to write ahead of writing. |

from *Early learning goals* (QCA 1999) and *Target statements for writing* (NLS 2000); see disk accompanying this book

# UNIT 1
# Foundation Stage – Reception: The Supermarket

**Target**: Invest writing with meaning; write simple labels
**Pupil target**: I can tell you about the signs and labels in our class supermarket.
**Outcome**: Lists and labels for supermarket in role-play area

## OBJECTIVES

**T1a** to recognise printed and handwritten words in a variety of settings …;
**T1b** that words can be written down again for a wide range of purposes;
**T11a** to understand that writing can be used for a range of purposes …;
**T11b** to understand that writing remains constant …;

**Early learning goals: communication, language and literacy**
- Enjoy listening to and using spoken and written language and readily turn to it in their play and their learning.
- Extend their vocabulary, exploring the meanings and sounds of new words.
- Use language to imagine and recreate roles and experiences.
- Use talk to organise, sequence and clarify thinking, ideas, feelings and events.
- Use their phonic knowledge to write simple regular words and make phonetically plausible attempts at more complex words.
- Attempt writing for different purposes, using features of different forms.

## Purpose and context

As part of a unit of work on the theme of 'food', the role-play area is to be converted into a supermarket. The children are involved in planning and setting this up and have undertaken a range of preparatory activities designed to activate their prior knowledge and heighten their awareness of print and information used in familiar packaging and also of the types of signs, labels and captions used to help shoppers locate items. Photographs have been taken of the main display features in the local supermarket, to which a visit has been arranged and during which children will be helped to compare the photographs with what they see in the shop, whilst shopping for a specified list of items required for a cooking activity.

## Session 1
### Shared writing
TEACHER DEMONSTRATION
- You will need a recipe related to a planned cooking activity. The recipe should be displayed so that the list of ingredients is prominent and the instructions written in simple sentences and in numbered order.
- Explain to the children that they are going to be doing some cooking. First they will be looking at the recipe to see what the ingredients are and to make a shopping list ready for the forthcoming visit to the supermarket.
- Display the recipe, ensuring that the list of ingredients is prominent.

> Here's the recipe for our cakes …
> Let's see what we need so that I can write a shopping list – then we'll remember everything when we go shopping. This is where it tells me what I need and down here it tells me what to do.

- Read the list item by item, whilst copying the ingredients onto the board.
- You may wish to involve the children in helping you with some initial letter sounds for spelling.
- Demonstrate checking your handwritten list against the items in the recipe. Draw attention to any specific features of the ingredients required, discussing with the children how this will involve consulting the packaging and displays carefully and reminding them what they know about familiar packages.

> Do you remember how we could tell from the packet whether it was cornflakes or branflakes? … We need to make sure that we buy **self-raising flour** … I wonder how we can make sure that we get the right sort of flour?

- Conclude by telling the children that they will be given copies of your list to help them when they go shopping.

## Experience

During their visit to the supermarket children will be supported by accompanying adults as they compare the photographs with the displays; use directional signs, eg **Home baking**, **Eggs**, to locate items and consult the shopping list and packaging to buy correct items.

## Plenary

TALK FOR WRITING

- Involve children in paired/small group discussion about the visit to the supermarket and how they used the different printed information to find their way round and locate the required items.
- Summarise their discussion in two sentences as a 'news' item for the noticeboard, talking aloud about what you are writing and involving the children in some of the decisions involved.

> I'm going to write two sentences about our trip and put it on the noticeboard. Now … what shall I say first? I think I'll write **On Tuesday we went to the supermarket**. as my first sentence. Who can tell me where to start writing? … I can't remember how to spell **Tuesday** – where can I look? … Who can help me spell **to**? etc.

## Activity

*Note:* Prior to this, children should have been involved in shared reading of the recipe.

Groups of children make the cakes. The adult has prepared strips of cards on which the ingredients are shown and these are used during the session to compare with the packaging, locate the right item, etc. The recipe is displayed with the instructions expressed in simple sentences in numbered order. The adult makes a point of using the vocabulary: **first**, **next**, **last**, and of drawing attention to the numbers preceding each instruction.

## Session 2
### Shared writing
TEACHER SCRIBING

- Explain to the children that you are all going to start planning the role-play supermarket. Briefly display the recipe you used to compile the shopping list.
- Remind them of the layout features – the list of *what you need* and the instructions for *what you do*. Now you are going to start planning the role-play area together, starting with the list of what you need.

> I've got a big sheet of paper here for us to make the list of what we need, so first I'm going to write the heading **What we need**.

- Write the heading, involving the children in some of your decisions as a writer, eg where to start, spacing of words, aspects of letter formation and spelling. Then ask the children, in pairs, to discuss the things that will be needed in order to set up the supermarket.
- Scribe the appropriate suggestions on the sheet, drawing attention to the layout of the list and involving them in some of the 'writerly' decisions as above.

### Independent work
- The children draw or write their own lists.
- The children consult your list and begin to find some of the items noted (with adult support as needed).

### Plenary
Reread the list, helping the children to match items to the correct objects.

## Session 3
### Shared writing
TEACHER DEMONSTRATION

- Explain that now you have got the list of things you need, the next thing you need to do is to write the instructions for what to do. As before, write the heading on the paper.
- With the teaching assistant, briefly model a discussion about what needs to be done, then involve children in the discussion, helping them to identify appropriate actions but not worrying about the order in which they are noted. Ask the teaching assistant to jot down the ideas as notes on the flip chart.
- Now tell them that you are going to write down their instructions and that you need to make sure that you do everything in the right order.

> Do you remember, when we made the cakes the other day we had to make sure that we did everything in the right order? The instructions about what to do in the recipe told us what to do **first**, what to do **next** and what to do **last**. Who can remember what else we had on the instructions to help us to do things in the right order? … That's right, there were **numbers** at the beginning of each sentence. I'm going to use numbers to help us. Now, let me see what we've got first here in our notes … it says 'Put tins and packets on shelves.' We can't do that **first** because we haven't got the shelves ready. The first thing we'll need to do is arrange the furniture. … Have we got a note about that? … Oh yes, it says down here get the shelves ready. I'm going to write that as the **first** instruction.

- Make a short list of simple instructions in this way, drawing attention to the difference between letters and numbers and the vocabulary **first**, **next**, **last**. Model the rereading of each instruction to check for sense.

## Activity
Children are involved in the setting up of the role-play area, with adult support in referring to the list of requirements and instructions for action.

## Plenary
TALK FOR WRITING
- Involve the children in paired/shared discussion about what has been involved in setting up the supermarket.
- As in Session 1, summarise this and record as an item for the class noticeboard.

## Session 4
### Shared writing
TEACHER DEMONSTRATION
The supermarket is ready, but now needs signs and labels. Display some of the photographs of the signs and labels in the local supermarket and demonstrate rewriting some of these onto strips of card which are to be used in your class shop. Involve children in some of the 'writerly' decisions as before. Demonstrate rereading and checking aspects of spelling and letter formation.

SUPPORTED COMPOSITION
Work with small groups of children in the role-play area, as they write their own signs and labels. Interventions to support their independent writing should be made, as appropriate, at the children's level.

## Plenary
- Select some of the children's written labels at differing levels of attainment and display them on the flip chart.
- Comment positively on the correct features of their writing.

> This is Jasprit's label – can you read it to us? Jasprit has written **bread**. Well done, Jasprit, you've got the 'b' at the beginning … Shaynene has got the 'j' at the beginning of **jam** and the 'm' at the end …

## Session 5
### Talk for writing

● Adults work alongside the children in the role-play area introducing/developing key language structures and vocabulary.

● Use phrases such as **please**, **thank you**, **may I …?** and model questions such as **Would you like a basket, sir?** and **Where can I find the sausages?** Demonstrate use of a shopping list of items to buy.

● Observe, model and encourage children to use signs/labels to locate items. Make explicit the reading and writing link.

> Good morning, I'm going to make sandwiches for my children's tea tonight, so I've made a list of things I need. Can you help me to find them, please? Here's my shopping list … now what does it say first … oh yes, **bread**. Can you help me to find the bread please?
> Where's the sign for bread?
> What letter does it begin with?

### Plenary

● Children in pairs discuss what they bought/did or helped the adult to buy when in the role-play area.

● As before, record children's achievements in a sentence such as 'We can use our labels to find what we need.'

## What next?

The next session would involve writing a promotional poster to tell others about the role-play supermarket. There are also many opportunities for links with different areas of learning with this role-play area, particularly mathematical development. Texts such as *The Pet Sale* by Mick Inkpen, *The Shopping Basket* by John Burningham or *Going Shopping* by Sarah Garland can be used to support this. The children could also be involved in sorting and classifying foods and articulating preferences linking with knowledge and understanding of the world.

# UNIT 2
# Foundation Stage – Reception:
# The Bear Hunt

**Targets**: Think about what to write ahead of writing. Begin to write simple sentences
**Pupil target**: I can talk about my ideas and write a sentence about them.
**Outcome**: A class story

## OBJECTIVES

| | |
|---|---|
| **T7** | to use knowledge of familiar texts to re-enact or re-tell to others, recounting the main points in correct sequence; |
| **T14** | to use experience of stories, poems and simple recounts as a basis for independent writing … and through shared composition with adults; |
| **S1** | to expect written text to make sense and check for sense if it does not; |

**Early learning goals**
- Extend their vocabulary, exploring the meanings and sounds of new words.
- Use language to imagine and recreate roles and experiences.
- Use talk to organise, sequence and clarify thinking, ideas, feelings and events.
- Explore and experiment with sounds, words and texts.
- Retell narratives in the correct sequence, drawing on language patterns of stories.
- Use their phonic knowledge to write simple regular words and phonetically plausible attempts at more complex words.
- Attempt writing for different purposes, using features of different forms.
- Write their own names and other things such as labels and captions and begin to form simple sentences, sometimes using punctuation.

## Purpose and context

Through shared reading, children have become familiar with the text, *We're Going on a Bear Hunt* by Michael Rosen and Helen Oxenbury. It is particularly important that the children are familiar with the repetitive phrases used in the text.

## Session 1
### Talk for writing
- Involve the children in a dramatised retelling of the story. They are going to go on their own pretend journey or bear hunt, thinking hard about the story they have been reading and seeing if they can remember all the things that the family had to pass and go through on their way to the bear's cave. The tricky bit is that they have to try to get the events in the right order.
- In the retelling, place great emphasis on the physical events and their sequence.

### Shared writing
TEACHER DEMONSTRATION
- Explain to the children that you are going to write a list of the physical features found in the text in the correct sequence. You want them to help you to remember the order in which things happened.

- As you write, think aloud and involve them in some of the decisions you need to make as a writer (layout of list, initial and final phonemes, spelling of CVC words, etc.).
- To help them to get the events in order you could use the sound effects as prompts, eg:

**Long, wavy grass**
**A deep, cold river**
**Thick, oozy mud**
**A big, dark forest**
**A snowstorm**
**A narrow, gloomy cave**

Reread the list with the children.

## Independent work

This could include:
- the children drawing pictures to act as visual prompts for each of the events;
- independent reading of the text;
- the teaching assistant retelling the story with a group, involving children in following the list of events;
- the children using percussion instruments or body percussion to make the sounds which match the events on the list.

## Plenary

TALK FOR WRITING
- Involve the children in paired and then whole class discussion about their favourite part of the journey.
- Summarise their discussion by demonstrating the writing of two sentences that record this and refer to the sequence of the story, eg **We've thought hard about the order of the story of the bear hunt. Our favourite part of our journey was going through the long wavy grass and making the swishy, swashy sounds**.
- Reread the sentences, involving the children as appropriate in checking for sense, use of capital letters and full stops and spelling of sight words.

## Session 2
### Shared writing
TEACHER SCRIBING
- Display a backdrop or story map of the setting that has visual prompts of the physical features in sequence.
- Explain that you are making a plan to help you remember the story and that you think a map is the best way. You want the children to help you to write the titles for the physical features – the same ones as you made into a list.
- Scribe the names of the physical features and relevant sound effects onto the map based on children's recall and response, thinking aloud and involving children as before.

### Independent work
TALK FOR WRITING
- The children can use the story map/setting and characters (made from card, Playmobil/Lego people or dolls) to re-enact and retell the story. (This is an opportunity for observation of children's knowledge of the story and ability to retell in the correct sequence.)

● Supported oral composition: the children could retell the story, prompted by an adult to add the repetitive links or chorus in order to sustain the sequence.

## Plenary

A group of children can retell the story using the map and characters. The rest of the children listen and watch carefully to see if the sequence of events is correct.

## Session 3
### Shared writing

Explain to the children that you are going to focus on the last part of the story by using four pictures that illustrate what the family do when they meet the bear.

TEACHER DEMONSTRATION

Tell the children that you are going to write a sentence to accompany the first picture. It is very important that this should explain what is happening in the picture.

> I need to look really carefully at the picture and think about what I can see … I can see the family arriving at the front door and then they open it and run up the stairs. So, what shall I write … I need to remember to write as if the people in the picture are telling the story, so I'll start with **We**. I'll just try saying my sentence first before I write it … **We open the door and run up the stairs**. … I think that sounds right so I'm going to write that.

TEACHER SCRIBING

● Ask the children to look carefully at the second picture and to try to think of a sentence about it. Take suggestions, recasting their contributions into sentences as necessary and choosing one succinct idea for the next sentence to be written. Scribe the sentence, modelling its oral rehearsal before you write it.

● Conclude by rereading the two sentences, reinforcing the features of a sentence.

### Independent work

Ask the children to think about what they would do if they met a bear and where they would hide.

● Use the illustrations from the text and let the children have a go at writing their own sentences that explain what is happening.

- The children could draw a sequence of up to four pictures of their own that show what they would do if they met a bear, and have a go at writing underneath.
- They could look at the final picture then decide where they might hide, draw a picture to show this and have a go at writing a sentence about it.

I hid under my bed

(I sellotaped the door shut)

## Plenary
### TALK FOR WRITING
Help the children to feed back from their activities by referring to their pictures and sentences. Make a point of praising contributions which are in sentences and, as necessary, recast their contributions as sentences.

## Session 4
### Context/Purpose
Through shared reading, children will have become familiar with the story *This is the Bear and the Scary Night* by Sarah Hayes and Helen Craig.

### Shared writing
#### TALK FOR WRITING/TEACHER DEMONSTRATION
- Begin the session by retelling the story using key pictures as prompts, then refer to the last four pages of the book where the bear tells his story.
- Read this aloud, asking questions to ensure that the children focus on this part of the story very closely.

> **This is the bear
> who started to tell
> how he flew through the air
> and how he fell** What does he mean he flew through the air and then fell? How did this happen? Who made him fly through the air?
> **and how he floated** Where did he float?
> **and how he was saved** Who saved him?
> **and how he was
> terribly, terribly brave** Why was he brave?

- Tell the children that you are all going to think of some words that tell you how the boy was feeling when he lost his bear.
- Ask them to talk in their pairs about how he felt and take feedback, explaining that you are going to make a note of some of the important *words* (not sentences) that tell you how the boy felt.
- With the help of the teaching assistant as a contributor, add to their ideas so that there is a choice of words/bank of vocabulary to draw on: **sad, upset, cross, worried, frightened**, etc.
- Conclude the session by demonstrating the writing of the sentence: **When the boy lost his bear he felt sad.**, rehearsing it aloud before you begin writing and then thinking aloud about your 'writerly' decisions – involve children in some of these.
- Ask the children to reread the sentence with you, checking for sense, punctuation, initial and final phonemes, etc.

## Independent work

The children could draw the picture of the boy losing his bear and have a go at writing their own sentence. Provide the sentence starter where needed.

## Plenary

Help some children to read their sentences aloud, asking the rest of the children to listen carefully to see if the sentences make sense and help children to ask questions about the sentences. Model this process with the teaching assistant.

> Did you remember to put a full stop at the end? … What was the last word in your sentence – **sad** – Oh yes, can you tell me how you have spelt **sad**? … etc.

## Session 5
### Talk for writing
TEACHER SCRIBING

- Refer to the list of words compiled in the previous session and read them through with the children.
- Tell them that today, you want them to think about how they would feel if they lost their toy.
- Ask them to share information about their favourite toy and how they might feel if they lost it.
- Help children to phrase their feedback into sentences. Choose some successful examples and scribe them for the children, rerunning their sentence aloud before you write and asking the children to help you with aspects of the writing.

### Independent work
The children could draw a picture of their bear/favourite toy discussed earlier and have a go at writing how they would feel if they lost it. For some children, a sentence starter may be given.

### Plenary
As Session 4

## What next?
The unit could be developed into further sessions where children look at the kind of cards and advertisements posted for lost items. After considering the kind of information needed, they could prepare labels for a toy giving the name of the owner, address and telephone number. This could lead into the writing of a final verse to be added to the story, *This is the Bear and the Scary Night*, eg:

**This is the bear**
**Who now wears a label,**
**So that if he gets lost**
**And if people are able**
**They can look round his neck**
**In order to check**
**Who the bear belongs to.**

# UNIT 3
# Foundation Stage – Reception:
# The Exhibition

**Target**: Label information appropriately
**Pupil target**: We can write labels for the pictures in our exhibition.
**Outcome**: Set up and label exhibition

## OBJECTIVES

| | |
|---|---|
| **T12** | to write labels or captions for pictures and drawings; |
| **S1** | to expect written text to make sense and check for sense if it does not; |
| **W6** | to read on sight the 45 high frequency words to be taught by the end of YR, from Appendix List 1; |

**Early learning goals: communication, language and literacy**
- Write their own names and other things such as labels and captions and begin to form simple sentences, sometimes using punctuation.
- Extend their vocabulary, exploring the meaning and sounds of new words.

***Note:*** Other links can be made with early learning goals for Knowledge and Understanding of the World and also Creative Development.

## Purpose and context

As part of a unit of work on the theme of 'Local Buildings', the children are preparing an interactive exhibition to inform interested adults and friends about buildings in the local community. The teacher has prepared enlarged photographs of some local buildings. These will be used to facilitate discussion and as a basis for observational drawings. Models and collage pictures will be made and displayed, together with captions to explain them to the exhibition visitors. Posters will advertise the event and personal invitations will be sent to relatives and friends of the exhibitors. On the day itself, children will act as guides, explaining the exhibits to the visitors.

## Session 1
### Talk for writing
- Explain that it would be really useful for people who live in the area to learn more about the local buildings and what they are for. Explain the word **exhibition** and suggest that they should arrange one in the classroom and invite parents/carers and friends to come along.
- Show them some photographs of local buildings.
- The first step will be to decide which of the photographs to use.
- Tell the children that you think you have taken far too many, and some of them are not very interesting or important buildings.
- Select one of the photos and model the process of deciding whether it would be a good one to use in the exhibition.

> Now let me see … there's a picture here of the corner shop. I think this is a building that lots of people use. It's an important building, because people go there to do their shopping. I wonder if people would like to see this in our exhibition? Yes, I've decided. We *will* put it in the exhibition, **because** lots of people go there. Did you notice that word – **because**? It's a good one to use when you're telling people **why**.

- Select another photograph and ask the children to discuss it in pairs. Ask them first to decide whether they want to use it in the exhibition, and then say why.
- Remind them of the model given, using the word **because**.
- Then ask a few children to voice their responses, either praising the fact that children explain their reasons, or prompting them to do so and modelling the use of the word **because**.

## Activity
TALK FOR WRITING

Children work in small groups with an adult to identify the buildings in the photographs, discuss their purposes, and decide which pictures to use, giving reasons.

## Plenary
TALK FOR WRITING

- Display the photographs in two sets – those generally agreed to be suitable for the exhibition and those rejected.
- With the teaching assistant, model a conversation in which you ask why a particular picture was selected or rejected and the teaching assistant replies, giving the children's reasons and using the **because** construction.
- Remind children that it is a good idea, when making decisions, to discuss the problem with a friend, and explain why you have decided to do something.
- The children are keeping a record of all their achievements. Demonstrate the writing of the sentence, 'We can explain why we do things, using the word **because**.'

## Session 2
### Shared writing
TEACHER DEMONSTRATION

- Remind the children that they have selected a set of photos to be displayed at the exhibition.
- Explain that the visitors will need to know first what the building is, then what people use the building for. They will therefore need to write a caption for each one, comprising this information. A few of the YR sight words are already displayed on Post-it notes, having been used in shared and guided reading.
- Select one of the photos and begin to demonstrate the process of composing a caption for it, pointing out that some of the Post-it words might be useful.

> Now, let me think, my first sentence needs to tell the visitors what the building is. I wonder how I could start? Perhaps I could write **It is the corner shop.** No, I think **This** might sound better – let me see **This is the corner shop.** – yes, that's nice and clear. I'm going to find some of those words on the Post-it notes, and the others I will have a go at myself. Will you help me practise the sentence again before I start to write it? Let's say it together …. I wonder how many words I need. Talk to your partner and decide how many words I am going to write.

- Then go on to ask which is the first word of the sentence and model the use of the word **collection**.
- Ask the children to decide, with their partners, which word says **this** and remove the Post-it note to the whiteboard to begin the sentence, asking a child to help decide on its position at the top left-hand side of the board.
- The words **This is the** are chosen from the Post-it collection, using the opportunity to reinforce knowledge of directionality and the concept of a word.
- Point out that spaces are needed between the words, so that when we reread it, we know which word is which.
- Write the word **corner** and then use the word **shop** to demonstrate the process of hearing the first phoneme in the word.

> Oh, that's interesting, I need to write two letters for that one phoneme.

- Next, tell the children that the sentence must start with a capital letter, and ask them to help find the capital 'T' on the alphabet chart or 'washing line'.
- Correct the first letter and ask a child to add the full stop at the end.
- Ask the children to reread the sentence together, while you point very deliberately at each word.

## Independent work

Children select a different photo and write the first sentence about it, combining the use of the Post-it notes and 'have a go' spelling.

## Plenary

- Read the sentence about one of the buildings and remind the children what is good about it, eg *'It tells the visitor what the building is, there are spaces between the words, and it starts with a capital letter and ends with a full stop.'*
- Ask the teaching assistant to read a sentence to the children. Do the children think it meets the same criteria?
- Ask the children to read their sentences aloud to a partner, pointing carefully as they read, and checking that the sentences meet the stated requirements. You may then choose to share one or two examples with the children, giving specific praise for the children's work against the same criteria.
- As before, demonstrate the writing of a sentence to summarise their achievements: 'We can write sentences to tell people about the photographs.'

## Session 3
### Shared writing
TEACHER SCRIBING

- Remind the children that the current objective is to write a caption for each of the photographs to be included in the exhibition.
- Reread the sentence from yesterday and explain that, to complete the caption, they need to give some more information. Then ask what additional information might be useful for the people who are coming to the exhibition.
- After children have discussed this in pairs, take some suggestions, saying what you like about each one.
- Select one idea and repeat it to the children, not yet framing it into a caption. Tell them that they now need to put those thoughts into one simple idea or sentence, then reread yesterday's sentence as a model.

This is the sentence I wrote yesterday: **This is the corner shop.** The sentence is short and simple. It tells us what we need to know, but it doesn't give us too much extra information. Our next sentence needs to do the same. Now, Peter suggests that we need to tell people that you can buy all sorts of food at the corner shop. Turn to your partner and see if you can put those ideas into a simple sentence, like the one I wrote yesterday.

- Listen to a range of suggestions and select one. If necessary, praise the ideas offered and frame them into a simple sentence, then ask the children to repeat the sentence and decide which is the first word. Scribe the sentence a word at a time, stopping several times to reread it and check that it sounds right so far. Deliberately miss out a key word such as **the**.
- Next, ask the children to reread the sentence and ask whether it makes sense. The children discuss in pairs what needs to be done to put it right. Then insert the missing word. Add the capital letter and the full stop.
- Ask the children to reread the two sentences about the corner shop. Point out that they have created a caption that consists of two sentences. Tell them that they are going to read *just* the first sentence. How will they know when to stop reading? They read the first sentence together.
- Ask a child to draw a coloured ring around the first sentence, then the children read and mark the second sentence in the same way. Remind them that the two sentences together form a caption, which tells the visitors to the exhibition what the building *is* and what it is *for*.

## Talk for writing and independent work
- Give the children the same photograph they worked with before, and the sentence that they have already written.
- Explain that they are going to add another sentence that gives a bit more information about their building.
- Help the whole group read each of the sentences aloud.
- In pairs, the children talk about what extra information they will give, and they help each other frame the idea into a sentence.
- Select one of the sentences and either praise the fact that it does constitute a sentence, or frame the words into a sentence for the benefit of the whole group.
- The children then write their sentences independently. (NB The expectations of each child regarding spelling have already been made clear, eg some children know that they must write at least one initial letter for each word, others write at least the first and last letter of every word, and others are expected to represent all the phonemes in the words.) If necessary, return to write a transcription of the child's writing on a Post-it note attached to the child's work.

## Plenary
- Display the children's captions. Refer to them and select two examples at different levels of attainment, praising the specific achievements of each child.
- As before, demonstrate the writing of a sentence to summarise achievement: 'We can write captions for the pictures in our exhibition.'

*Note:* Over a period of time, the children could produce word-processed versions of their captions, using a Clicker grid or concept keyboard. These can be used to create a guide book for visitors to the exhibition or, after the event, to create a book for the children's use entitled 'Local Buildings'.

## Shared reading

Now that the purpose and context of the writing have been established, a Big Book which features simple captions can be used over the next few days to consolidate and extend the understanding about sentences and captions gained from the shared and independent writing experiences above.

Also over the next few days, children are given opportunities to use the photographs as a basis for model-making, collage pictures, observational drawing, building using construction kits and blocks, etc. This will also facilitate mathematical discussion about shape and position.

## Session 4
### Shared writing
TALK FOR WRITING/TEACHER DEMONSTRATION

- Remind the children of the forthcoming exhibition and what has been achieved so far in preparation for it. Since the last shared writing session the children have made a range of pictures and models.
- Tell the children that the visitors would be interested to know *how* these were made.
- Show the children a model/collage picture (perhaps one that you have made) and explain a little about how it was made, using the words **first**, **then** and **finally**.
- On the whiteboard, display three empty squares, labelled **First**, **Then** and **Finally**.
- Explain that you want to write about how you made the model, but would like their help in planning what to say.

> The people who come to our exhibition will have lots of different things to look at, so they won't have time to read a long piece of writing.
> I thought I'd write three simple sentences, telling people what I did first, what I did after that – and what I did last of all. … I'm going to draw three pictures in these boxes, to make a plan for the sentences I need to write.
> These are the words I'm going to start my sentences with – I've written them out, ready to use – **First** for the first important thing I did, and **Then** for the next important thing I did. And for my last sentence I'm going to use a special word that means 'last of all'. Here it is – it says **Finally**.
> I did lots of things before I really got going on my model – I washed my hands and I rolled my sleeves up and I put on an apron – but I don't think people will really want to read that. It's not very interesting – and anyway, I do that every time I make something at school – so what do you think is the first *important* thing I need to say?

- Ask them to discuss with a partner what they think you should draw in the 'First' square.
- In taking feedback from the children, reiterate the fact that, although you did a great deal in preparation for the model-making, you do not want to include this in the writing.
- Select one idea as the basis for the first sentence, eg choosing the materials to be used, then draw a very quick sketch to represent it. Follow the same pattern for the rest of the session, until the three key sentences are represented by three quick sketches in the planning frame.
- Ask the children to tell their partner briefly how they made their model. Remind them that they don't want to include much detail, so they are going to make a picture plan for three important things they will need to write. The children then turn to a partner and decide what the first *important* thing on their plan is going to be.

- Take a range of suggestions and praise one that gets straight to the point. Then ask the children to check with their partner whether their first idea is important enough to be the first picture.
- Tell them that today they are going to make a picture plan for their three sentences, and remind them that the 'Finally' box must show the last thing they did to complete the model/picture.

## Independent work

The children are provided with a three-box planning frame, and make a 'picture plan' for three sentences about their model/picture. The teacher explains that the three pictures must:

- represent three *important* moments in the process;
- be in a logical order.

## Plenary

- Display the three pictures from your plan, but in the wrong order. The 'First', 'Then' and 'Finally' labels are displayed separately.
- Look at each picture in turn, reminding children what is depicted. Then ask the children what is wrong and help them to re-order them under the appropriate headings. Remind the children that the order of the sentences is important, and that the 'Finally' box must show what they did to complete the model. Ask them to tell a partner what they drew in their last box and check whether it was the last thing they did to complete their model or picture.
- Display the heading words prominently, and remind children that they will be useful words, particularly when they are writing about a series of things that happened one after the other.

## Session 5
### Shared writing
TEACHER SCRIBING

- Display your own 'picture plan' on the whiteboard. Explain that the children are going to help you to write three sentences, saying three important things about how the model was made.
- Remind the children that there are three pictures and three sentences are needed, saying three important things about the model.
- Think aloud to compose the first sentence: 'First I collected all the things I needed.'
- Decide which is the first word, then model the writing of the sentence, thinking aloud about the capital letter and also the direction and spacing, and rerunning the sentence several times to check that it makes sense.
- Add the full stop, then tell the children what is happening in the second picture, reminding them that there needs to be one sentence – one complete idea – about this picture.
- Ask children to talk to a partner and compose one sentence about the picture.
- Select one contribution, shaping it if necessary into a sentence and reminding them that you are keeping it short and simple.
- Scribe the sentence, running it over more than one line and putting the full stop at the end of the line.
- Ask the children to read together up to the full stop then decide, with a partner, whether it is in the right place. 'Does that sound right? Does it sound finished?' etc., then they reread the whole sentence and put the full stop at the end.
- Quickly model the writing of the last sentence correctly, reiterating all the key points already made.

## Independent work

The children work with a partner and, using their picture plans, rehearse their three key sentences orally before writing a sentence under each picture. When they have finished, they are asked to read their sentences to a partner and check whether they have left spaces between words, begun with a capital letter and ended with a full stop.

## Plenary

Choose an example of three sentences that are not correctly punctuated and write it in large print on the board. Announce that you have chosen this child as 'writer of the day' because there are so many good things about this writing. List several good points about the child's writing, drawn from the criteria above.

> Something you need to know about good writers is that they are always trying to find ways to make their writing even better. We're going to try to think of one idea to help Sharanjit do that now. Do you remember that she wrote three sentences about her model? How many full stops should she have then? ... Let's read Sharanjit's three sentences and decide where she could put the three full stops. Remember that when we get to the full stop, the idea should be finished – it should make sense. ... So, Sharanjit, do you want to come and put the full stop in now?

Praise the children for their work and write the sentence: 'We can write sentences about our models.'

*Note:* This could be followed by two or three shared reading sessions, examining the features of invitations, notes and messages, using enlarged versions of 'real' messages, etc. or possibly in the context of a story, eg *The Jolly Postman* series by Allan Ahlberg and *Don't Forget to Write* by Martina Selway.

## Session 6
### Shared writing
TEACHER DEMONSTRATION

Explain to the children that they need to write and tell people about the exhibition and that you have already prepared an invitation which you have photocopied, ready for them to take home and also to offer friends in school. Display an enlarged copy of this and read it to the children, explaining the choice of layout, vocabulary and punctuation.

- Explain that before the invitation can be delivered to the teacher in Year 1, you are going to add a sentence at the bottom, because you don't want her to miss the model you made of the Short Street Library. So you are going to write 'Remember to look at my model of the library.'
- Rehearse the sentence aloud and model the writing as before. The children help to check that it makes sense, and add the capital letter and full stop. Complete the invitation by signing your name.
- Suggest that each of the children might like to add a comment to their invitation before they take it home, and ask them to discuss this with a partner. They need to decide on the recipient and also think about what they might like to add.
- Take a range of suggestions, then remind them that they will need to put what they want to say into a short sentence. The children then rehearse their sentence aloud with their partner. Having listened to some of their suggestions, remind them that their idea should be short and simple, without too many **and**s, and ask them to check this once more with their partner.

**Come to our exciting exhibition!**

Learn all about the interesting buildings in our neighbourhood.

We have photographs, models, and all sorts of pictures for you to see!

**Where?** In YR Classroom.

**When?** On Monday 20th and Tuesday 21st November from 2.45 till 3.15 pm

**SEE YOU THERE!**

## Independent work

The children put their personal comment at the bottom of their invitation and illustrate it with pictures of the buildings.

## Plenary

Remind the children of, and congratulate them upon, all the preparations they have made for the exhibition. There are just a few finishing touches that need to be made. The visitors will need somebody to take them around and explain all the exhibits. The children will therefore be 'official guides', and will be making their own identity badges. This is a very important job and over the next few days, children will undergo special 'training'. This will include making sure they can read the main captions and notices and those about their own exhibits. There will be a practice run, when children from Year 1 will be invited to a preview of the exhibition, before it is opened to the public.

## What next?

- The children undergo the 'training' as above, take responsibility for the final preparations, and show visitors around the exhibition. Pictures and notices can be 'recycled' after the event, to form books to be made available in the book area, and used in shared reading.
- The next unit of work might give children opportunities to investigate how buildings are constructed. They could interview a local builder about his work, set up an outdoor role-play area featuring sand play, building with large blocks, painting opportunities, vehicles as 'diggers', and so on. Children could be involved in planning, discussing, negotiating, instructing and explaining in pairs and small groups.
- Life-sized posters could be made, featuring tradespeople in different roles, with labels and notices advising children of appropriate clothing and equipment for each role.
- Safety notices and direction signs would need to be created, providing further opportunities for shared, guided and independent reading and writing. Both fiction and non-fiction texts could provide models for writing.

# Year 1

## Contents

# Introduction

When children enter Year 1, they already know a great deal about language and are able to express themselves in a variety of ways. The learning secured in the Foundation Stage will be developed and applied in a rich and varied range of literacy activities throughout this year. The NLS *Framework for teaching* objectives for Year 1 includes important reading, writing and word level objectives, which must be covered to support this progress.

The teaching units included in this guidance are designed to support the development of independent writing in a range of text types. The emphasis in every lesson is to ensure that a genuine purpose and context for the writing is established and that shared writing is used effectively to support children into independence. The units include examples of:

● teachers talking to children about the decisions they make as effective writers;
● children talking together about the writing task and the content of their pieces;
● children using dry-wipe boards to experiment and attempt sections of the text together before writing alone;
● teachers giving immediate feedback on early attempts to confirm or correct emerging conceptions about the writing process.

During the first year of school most children will use their knowledge of the conventions of our writing system to represent a range of ideas. It is important to plan and provide varieties of experiences to support and motivate children to write. In these units the purpose and context for writing includes responding to text introduced in the Literacy Hour and activities completed in information technology, science, geography and drama.

The six units have been selected to support your teaching to key writing targets and objectives. They include a range of text types to support learning: personal recount, instructional texts, traditional stories, reports and poetry. They focus on generating simple sentences, connecting simple sentences and organising ideas in a logical structure.

## Talk for writing

During shared writing it is important to provide opportunities for children to talk about the writing process and discuss the content of their writing with others. These focused discussions help to clarify ideas, rehearse unfamiliar language structures and extend the range of vocabulary. Listening to children as they prepare to write will provide valuable insights which will be used to assess their progress and to support future planning.

## Sentence level activities

The six units are followed by a set of sentence games and activities. These materials will encourage pupils to investigate how writing differs from speech, how sentences are constructed and how punctuation is used to support the reader.

By the end of Year 1, in writing, most children will have learned to:

| | |
|---|---|
| Phonics and spelling | <ul><li>Spell words with adjacent consonants, eg **drift**.</li><li>Attempt to spell unfamiliar words using a phonemic strategy (including analogy) and graphic knowledge.</li><li>Know main spelling choices for each vowel phoneme.</li><li>Spell 50 words in Y1/Y2 list in Appendix List 1 in the NLS *Framework*.</li></ul> |
| Handwriting | <ul><li>Form lower case letters correctly in a script that will be easy to join later.</li></ul> |
| Style: language effects | <ul><li>Begin to use words appropriate to different text forms, eg story, reports or simple instructions.</li></ul> |
| Style: sentence construction | <ul><li>Write simple sentences independently.</li><li>Write questions and statements appropriately.</li></ul> |
| Punctuation | <ul><li>Use capital letters and full stops when punctuating a single simple sentence.</li><li>Begin to use question marks.</li></ul> |
| Purpose and organisation | <ul><li>Write a recount or narrative. Begin to break up the series of events with connectives other than **and**.</li><li>Build on YR – write to communicate meaning – simple recounts, stories that can be re-read, with basic beginning, middle and ending.</li><li>Write simple instructions in correct order.</li><li>Label information appropriately.</li></ul> |
| Process | <ul><li>Use language and structures from reading when writing.</li><li>Assemble information and ideas from own experience as a basis for writing, as well as writing questions prior to reading/writing.</li><li>Begin to rehearse sentences before writing and re-read during and after writing.</li></ul> |

from *Target statements for writing* (NLS 2000);
see disk accompanying this book

# UNIT 4
# Y1 Term 1: Where's My Teddy?

**Target:** Write simple sentences using the personal pronoun I
**Pupil target:** I can write a sentence starting with I.
**Outcome:** 'Story' based on personal experience – simple three-sentence recount
**Range:** Stories with familiar settings

## OBJECTIVES

| | |
|---|---|
| **T5** | to describe story settings and incidents and relate them to own experience and that of others; |
| **T9** | to write about events from personal experience linked to a variety of familiar incidents from stories; |
| **S4** | to write … simple sentences and to re-read recognising whether or not they make sense; |
| **S9** | to use a capital letter for the personal pronoun 'I' …; |
| **W6** | to represent in writing the three phonemes in CVC words …; |
| **W11** | to spell common irregular words from Appendix List 1; |

## Purpose and context

Writing will arise from reading stories and discussing experiences about losing something precious. Possible starting points could be:

- reading the story *Where's My Teddy?* by Jez Alborough;
- the teacher telling a story based on their own experience about losing something;
- the teacher 'finding' a little teddy and big teddy in the classroom, asking children how it got there;
- the teacher in role as 'Eddy' recounting what happened to him when he lost his teddy in the wood.

## Session 1
### Talk for writing

- Tell a simple story about something you have lost, eg The day I lost my ring ….
- Finish before the end, and get the children to think about where you might have found it again.
- Talk about the best way to end the story.

## Session 2
### Shared writing
TEACHER DEMONSTRATION

Demonstrate writing the first two sentences of the story. (The teacher needs to have composed these before writing, using the story just told: I lost my wedding ring. I felt very sad.)

> I'm going to have three sentences in my story. When I have written
> each sentence I'm going to put a tick at the bottom of the page. You can help
> me check. I am using a capital 'I' because we always use a capital 'I' when we are
> writing about ourselves. … I have written my first idea, so I'm going to put a
> full stop at the end. Let me read that back to myself to see if it makes
> sense. …Yes that's alright, so I'll put a tick at the
> bottom of the page.

> Now I am going to write my next
> sentence. Let me think about what I want to write.
> I've already said I've lost my wedding ring, now I want to say
> how I felt. Well, I remember that I felt really sad. How can I put that
> into a sentence? … I felt very sad. I'm going to remember to start with
> a capital 'I'. … Now. I'll read that through … and put a tick at the bottom
> of the page to show I have finished another sentence. Now I need to
> read all these sentences again to see if my story makes
> sense. It sounds right, so now you can help me
> write my last sentence.

TEACHER SCRIBING
- Ask the children to help you with the final sentence. Ask them to suggest where you found your ring.
- The children offer suggestions.
- Take one idea and reinforce what a sentence is.

> You said in the garden. I could say I found it in the
> garden. Which one of those sounds like a sentence?

- Ask the children what the first word is, and how it should be written (capital I).
- Involve the children in spelling some words using phonic skills and knowledge of high frequency words.
- Reread all three sentences together.

## Independent work
This could include:
- re-enacting the story with props;
- working with the teaching assistant, suggesting a setting and an object that is lost, and the children making up their own story;
- the children recording their own experiences or retelling the story on tape using three sentences;
- cutting up sentences from the shared text into individual words and asking the children to re-assemble into sentences.

## Plenary
Play one of the tapes, asking the class to listen carefully for the three sentences.

## Session 3

### Talk for writing

- Ask the children to talk to their partners about something they have lost.
- Then the teacher scaffolds the talk by asking three specific questions: 'What did you lose? How did you feel? Where did you find it?'
- Model the answers using sentences, eg child says 'my puppy', teacher says 'I can change that into a sentence … I lost my puppy.'
- Demonstrate what a sentence is, eg:

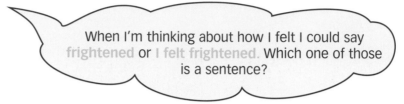

When I'm thinking about how I felt I could say frightened or I felt frightened. Which one of those is a sentence?

- Ask the children to check with their partner that they have got three ideas: I lost …, I felt …, I found ….

### Supported composition

- Children have dry-wipe boards (one between two). Ask them to think about the thing that they are going to write about having lost.
- The children take a turn each to write the name of the thing on their dry-wipe board. More able could write the sentence, I lost my….
- Demonstrate the difference between a word and a sentence.
- Take a couple more ideas from children's dry-wipe boards and ask them to put their idea into the sentence verbally, I lost my….

### Independent work

All the children write their own story using the three sentence structure and the personal pronoun I with appropriate provision for support and extension (ask the children to put a tick at the bottom of their page each time they complete a sentence).

### Plenary

- Have the children met the target? Some children share their recount, while the others listen for the following:
  - Is it about the child themselves?
  - Can they spot the three sentences? Ask them to put their hands up at the end of each sentence.
  - Did they start each sentence with I? What did they need to remember when they were writing I?
- Ask the children to respond by asking a further question of the reader, eg Did that really happen? Was your mum cross when you lost it?

### What next?

- Choose another text to use as a starting point and ask the children to write a story based on their own experience, eg going to school, going to the doctor, etc.
- Move the children on to using simple connectives to signal chronology, eg First I …, After that, I …, etc.

# UNIT 5
# Y1 Term 1: How to Use a Printer

**Target:** Write instructions in a series of simple sentences
**Pupil target:** I can write some sentences to give instructions.
**Outcome:** Instructions for controlling a machine, eg how to print your work from the computer
**Range:** Instructions

## OBJECTIVES

| | |
|---|---|
| **T13** | to read and follow simple instructions, e.g. for classroom routines …; |
| **T16** | to write and draw simple instructions … for everyday classroom use, e.g. in role play area, for equipment; |
| **S4** | to write captions and simple sentences, and to re-read, recognising whether or not they make sense, e.g. missing words, wrong word order; |
| **S5** | to recognise full stops and capital letters when reading, and name them correctly; |
| **S6** | to begin using the term sentence to identify sentences in text; |
| **S7** | that a line of writing is not necessarily the same as a sentence; |
| **W6** | to represent in writing the three phonemes in CVC words …; |
| **W11** | to spell common irregular words from Appendix List 1; |

**ICT Scheme of work**

Unit 1F: Understanding instructions and making things happen. Writing instructions in order to control a machine could come at the end of a whole series of practical work as suggested in the IT scheme of work, e.g. using a tape recorder to record and play back sound; giving spoken instructions to move from one point to another; making a floor turtle follow a planned path. The emphasis in the IT teaching and learning would be on the importance of sequence and its effect on outcome, and that instructions can be recorded for replication and amendment.

## Purpose and context

Writing will arise from practical experience as part of the ICT curriculum. This teaching unit involves using a computer and printer and controlling a sequence of instructions to print a piece of work. Experiences children will have had before the writing (these could also be follow-up activities for groups during the week):
- talking through process of how to use the printer, demonstrating each step to the children;
- opportunities to try out what has been taught for themselves;
- writing labels for the different parts of the computer. Make sure that they can recognise and read the labels, eg play a game where they have to stick the labels onto the right part of the computer (printer, switch, paper tray, mouse, cursor, tool bar, 'print' button).

## Session 1
### Talk for writing
- Introduce the purpose and audience. Explain to the children that they have been using the printer to print out their work, but you think it would be a good idea to have some instructions by the computer to remind them what to do.
- Have the computer ready, with text displayed on the screen. Get one child to demonstrate the process. Give a commentary whilst they are doing the actions, eg 'Now Sam is switching on the printer, now he is moving the cursor to the "print" button' etc., introducing the idea of a sequence of actions.

● Repeat the process and involve several children, each taking a turn to show one step, to get across the idea that there are steps to be followed.

● Would it matter if things were done in a different order? eg Try clicking on the 'print' symbol before the printer is switched on. What happens?

● After they have finished, the children each say what they did to reinforce the sequence.

● Explain that when you are writing an instruction, you don't need to say 'Sam did this …'. You just need the instruction itself, eg 'It's like giving an order! Do this …' (get children to wag their fingers and give an order to their partner). 'Turn to your partner and try giving an order!'

● Ask each of the children who did one of the 'steps' to have a go at changing their step from a recount of what they did to an instruction that anyone could follow.

● The children could talk in pairs to practise changing the 'steps' into the language of instructions.

## Independent work

This could include:

● groups working with other types of machine and practising giving instructions for someone else to follow;

● labelling parts on a picture/diagram of the computer;

● sequencing pictures of each step and talking through the sequence.

## Session 2
### Shared writing
TEACHER DEMONSTRATION

● Explain to the children that they thought about instructions for using the printer last time. Now they are going to start writing those instructions down so that they can have something to remind them what to do. Quickly recap the instructions, getting the children who were involved last time to stand up and remind the group what they did.

● Demonstrate writing the title and the first step of the instructions, based on what the children did in the previous session. You should have a clear idea of the sentences before you write, and talk through what you are doing, how you are making choices about words to use, spellings, etc. Use a fairly narrow piece of paper to write on (as if prepared for writing a list). Make sure that at least one 'step' in the instructions runs on to the next line.

> I am going to start to write a set of instructions for printing your work. I will need a title so that we know what these instructions are for: How to print your work. The first thing you need to do if you are printing your work is to switch on the printer. How can we turn that into an order? Say it to your partner and wag your finger. I am going to write Switch on the printer. What phonemes can you hear at the beginning of switch? What type of 's' shall I use? Why does it need to be a capital letter?

● Point out that instructions are different from other sorts of writing, because each time you write a new instruction you start a new line. This is to make it easier for other people to read and follow the instructions.

TEACHER SCRIBING

● Ask the children to decide what should be written for the next step, by turning to their partner and discussing their ideas. Remind them that when they are talking, they should make sure they think of a sentence that sounds like an order. Take suggestions from the children.

> I'm trying to decide whether to write Then you put the paper in the paper tray, or just Put the paper in the paper tray. They are both sentences, and they both make sense, but the second one sounds much more like an instruction.

● Say the sentence together and count the number of words. As you are writing the sentence, the children can keep count of the number of words. They can tell you when you have written all the words and therefore finished the sentence. Read the sentence to check that it makes sense.

## Session 3
### Shared writing

SUPPORTED COMPOSITION

● Give out dry-wipe boards and pen (one between two). Tell the children that they are going to discuss the next instruction with their partners and then write it on the dry-wipe board.
● When they have finished, talk about a specific spelling, eg 'I am going to use an idea that you have written to fill in the next instruction on my list, eg "Move the cursor to the print icon."' Write this.
● Return to a word the children have used and talk about a particular spelling, eg print. Segment into phonemes.
● This sentence will probably run onto a second line. Ask where the full stop should go. Point to the end of the line.

> Should it go here? Let's read what we have written. Did that sound right when we made the sentence stop at the end of the line? … No it didn't, because we hadn't finished the idea.

● Ask a child to help you put the full stop in the right place.
● Reread the instructions together all the way through.
● Tell the children that they are going to write the final two instructions on their own. Ask them to think about them with their partners.
● Take ideas and make sure the children have something like:

4. Click on the print icon.
5. Take your work out of the printer.

## Independent work

- Give out a sheet which has the three previous instructions already filled in, and spaces left for the children to complete the final two instructions.
- Children could write instructions to control another machine – one they use regularly at home or have used in class, eg How to play a video; How to record your voice on the tape recorder; How to move the floor turtle. Emphasise the purpose and audience, that they are writing instructions so that someone else can make this machine work.
- Children could draw their own sequence of pictures to demonstrate the steps needed, and add simple captions or labels.

### GUIDED WRITING

- Support the less able children by taking them to the computer and running through the steps again. Talk through step 4, then support them as they write, and again for step 5.
- Use the routine of counting the number of words in the sentence they want to write and then counting the words they have written to check whether their sentence is complete. Encourage them to reread what they have written as they write, and to write each instruction as a separate sentence.

---

Elizabeth

**How to print your work**

**1. Switch on the printer.**

**2. Put the paper in the printer.**

**3. Move the cursor to the 'print' button on the tool bar.**

**4.** _____
Click on the.
Print buttonon.

**5.** _____
take your Pa per'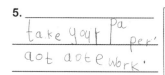
aot aote work.

---

## Plenary

- Ask the children whether they have written instructions that will actually help someone to make something work. Use an example – one child's writing – and work through the instructions. Were the instructions in the right order? Was anything missed out? Make changes or refinements as needed. Use the child's instructions to try printing work.
- Does the writing sound like instructions – giving orders? If the children have written as a recount, discuss what could be changed to make the writing sound more like instructions.
- Check for full stops at the ends of sentences. Ask the children to close their eyes and listen as you read a child's work aloud. Give a clue, eg 'There are five steps in these instructions, so you are listening for five sentences.' They could put up their hands when they think there should be a full stop.

## What next?

- Use the ICT scheme of work: the children could devise instructions to direct others to move from one place in the classroom to another. Write down the instructions. Try them out to check whether they work. Include the idea of the need for accurate measurements, precision, etc.
- Collect instruction books and simple manuals. Compare ways that instructions are presented, eg self-assembly furniture or Lego kits have a sequence of pictures instead of words.
- Ask children who have written instructions to give them to another child to follow when they have finished writing. Make any changes that are necessary as a result.

# UNIT 6
# Y1 Term 2: Cinderella

**Target:** Use a known story structure for own retelling, constructing a series of simple sentences
**Pupil target:** I can write a story using sentences.
**Outcome:** Retelling of the Cinderella story
**Range:** Traditional fairy stories

## OBJECTIVES

| | |
|---|---|
| **T14** | to represent outlines of story plots using, e.g. captions, pictures, arrows, to record main incidents in order, e.g. to make a class book, wall story, own version; |
| **T16** | to use some of the elements of known stories to structure own writing; |
| **S1** | to expect written text to make sense and to check for sense if it does not …; |
| **S5** | to continue demarcating sentences in writing, ending a sentence with a full stop; |
| **S6** | to use the term *sentence* appropriately to identify sentences in text …; |
| **S7** | to use capital letters for … names and for the start of a sentence; |
| **W9** | to spell common, irregular words from Appendix List 1; |

**Drama Scheme of work**

| | |
|---|---|
| **EN4a** | use language and actions to explore and convey situations, characters and emotion. |
| **EN4b** | create and sustain roles individually and when working with others. |
| **EN11a** | working in role. |

## Purpose and context

The story of Cinderella is introduced and read in the Literacy Hour and developed in Drama sessions. The children use a variety of activities to develop their understanding of the story. Some activities could include:

- hot-seating to develop understanding of character; freeze-frame to develop understanding of how characters interact and move the story on, and also showing the sequence of the story;
- role-on-the-wall in drama, where children have written a simple autobiography of their character and pinned it to a large map of Cinderella's village on the wall;
- writing letters to each other in role. By the time they come to write they have developed a strong idea of events and characters. They have also collected a long list of new vocabulary (eg Cinderella, ugly sisters, pumpkin, glass slipper, invitation), which is referred to when writing. Props and puppets have also been used to retell the story in whole class and group activities.

The role-play area might have been turned into a palace with children able to talk into a tape recorder in role.

## Session 1
### Talk for writing

This session focuses on the objectives of retelling the story using sentences and story language.

- Organise the class into groups of four. Give each group a set of story cards.

Now, I want you to put these pictures in the right order and I want you to tell the story from the pictures. When you tell the story, say it in sentences like: Once upon a time there lived a girl called Cinderella.

● Ask a group of children to come to the front, sequence pictures and retell the story in sentences.

## Session 2
### Shared writing
TEACHER DEMONSTRATION (WRITING USING A SIMPLE PLAN)

Do you remember yesterday how we told the story using picture cards? Today we're going to start writing the story. Before I write my story I've got to see if my ideas are in the right order. I'm going to write my story plan.

● Use a simple story plan proforma of beginning, middle and end to plot the story. Demonstrate the use of brief notes rather than full sentences, eg:

**Beginning** – Cinderella does housework, ugly sisters are cruel

**Middle** – invitation, sisters go to ball, Fairy Godmother makes spell, Cinderella goes to ball, Cinderella dances with Prince, loses slipper

**End** – Prince fits on slipper and marries Cinderella

Now I've written the ideas in the plan I can start writing. I shall start with the beginning. What happened in the beginning on my plan? Oh yes, Cinderella – housework and cruel ugly sisters. Now, what shall I say? I think I shall write Once upon a time, because that's how most fairy stories start.

● Point to story openers that you have collected and displayed on the wall.

> Once upon a time there lived a girl called
> Cinderella. I'll put a full stop there because that's the end of
> my sentence. Now, I'm going to read it again to see if I'm happy with it.
> Can you read it with me?
> Now, I want to say something about the ugly sisters. I'm remembering what
> Sarah said yesterday – She lived with her two ugly stepsisters.
> They were cruel to Cinderella. She did all the housework.
> 'I'm going to write those three sentences.

● When writing take a few opportunities to reinforce use of phonic strategies and high frequency words but don't stop at each word as it will halt the flow.

> Now, let's count how many sentences I've
> got in my beginning. I've got four. How could I check
> I've written in sentences? I'm going to start by counting the
> full stops. I've got four. A sentence also has a capital letter at
> the beginning, but how many capital letters
> can you see?

● Explain that there are more than four because capital letters are also used for names.

> We've got a good beginning to the story. It
> is written in four sentences, which have capital letters
> and full stops; it tells us about the things in our plan for the
> beginning of our story. Tomorrow, we'll write the middle
> and the end and you will have to help me.

## Independent work

Put the sentences onto strips of card. Ask the children to sort them into the correct order. Ask them if it makes any difference if one or more of the sentences is in a different order. Ask them to change the wording of the final sentence showing another way in which the sisters were cruel.

## Plenary

Take suggestions for the final sentences.

## Session 3
### Shared writing
TEACHER SCRIBING AND SUPPORTED COMPOSITION

● Show the children the story plan and opening four sentences from the previous lesson. Remind them of the task for the day.

Today we're going to write the middle and the end of our story. What happens in the middle of the story? Turn to your partner and say what happens in the middle of the story.

● Take ideas.

Now take what you've said and turn it into two sentences. … I'm going to write George's idea because that's what is in the plan. Let me say it to myself so that I've got it right. The ugly sisters got an invitation to the ball. Cinderella was sad because she couldn't go. I'm going to write that now. What do I have to remember? Yes, a capital 'T' for The.

● Write the two sentences.

Let's check we've got two sentences. I'll put a tick at the bottom of the page each time we find a sentence.

● Count the sentences and put two ticks at the bottom of the page.
● Hand out dry-wipe boards and pens. Look back at the plan to check where you are up to. Tell children to turn to their partners, think of the next thing that happens in the story and then write it on their boards.
● Look at a few examples and then choose one to write on the shared version.

I'm going to write Sunil's idea because that's what is in the plan. I'm going to write The Fairy Godmother waved her wand and Cinderella went to the ball.

● When writing Fairy Godmother show children how to use the list of characters on the wall to help with their spellings.

What else happens in the middle of the story? There's a problem for Cinderella isn't there? Let's look back at our plan to check.

● Children compose their next sentence(s), write on dry-wipe boards and then share with the class. Select which ones to use for the shared version, eg Cinderella danced with the prince. At midnight she ran away but she lost her glass slipper.

- Reread the story so far together.

> We've written the beginning and the middle,
> but how does the story end?

## Independent work

Ask the children to write two more sentences to end the story.

## Plenary

- Take a few moments to look through some of the story endings. Choose one and write it on the board. Reread the whole story together, checking that it makes sense. Count all the sentences and put ticks at the bottom of the page.

> Now, we've finished our story and we've got ….
> sentences. (Point to ticks.) Let's read it all together. Check
> with the plan that everything is included in the story.

- Return to the criteria for writing story and text and sentence level objectives and check together that these have been met.

## What next?

- Children can write simple plans for stories and use their plans to write stories. Write sentences in stories and put a tick at bottom of each page. Children can plan and write this and other fairy stories using a similar process. Make zigzag books, wall stories, etc. This could be done as independent work over a block of Literacy Hours or outside the Hour in sustained writing.
- Model the process of redrafting, eg take an example of one child's story plan and own writing. Read it through together and check that all the parts of the story have been included. Show how to add a bit more to the story if necessary.

# UNIT 7
# Y1 Term 2: Wheels

**Target:** To use the structure of a basic non-chronological report (heading, picture, facts) to organise own writing. To write factual sentences to describe a particular thing
**Pupil target:** I can write information about things in sentences. I can organise my work like an information book.
**Outcome:** Write a new page for the book, eg about scooter, roller blades
**Range:** Non-chronological report

## OBJECTIVES

**T25**  to assemble information from own experience, ... to use simple sentences to describe, based on examples from reading; to write simple non-chronological reports ...;

**S4**  to recognise full stops and capital letters when reading and understand how they affect the way a passage is read;

**S5**  to continue demarcating sentences in writing, ending a sentence with a full stop;

**S6**  to use the term *sentence* appropriately to identify sentences in text ...;

**S7**  to use capital letters for ... names and for the start of a sentence;

**W9**  to spell common irregular words from Appendix List 1;

**Science Scheme of work**
This work could come towards the end of Science Unit: 1E Pushes and pulls.

## Purpose and context

The children have been learning about movement. Their interest and new knowledge about the way things can move will be used as a starting point.

- Shared reading:
  - Read a non-fiction text which includes examples of machines and other objects using a variety of means to move, eg *Wheels, Wings and Other Things* by Rigby Star.
  - Talk about what makes the different vehicles in the book move, eg bicycles move by a person pushing the pedals, cars and trucks have engines, a sailing boat is moved by the wind.
  - Identify features which may appear on every page, ie heading, introductory sentence, photos and captions, 'Did you know?' box.
- Have a day when children can bring in scooters, roller blades, skateboards, etc. In the playground, play on the different toys, going slow, fast. Take photos to use in shared writing, and ensure there are three photos with a scooter: 1 Pushing off with foot; 2 Going downhill; 3 Wearing a helmet.

## Session 1
### Talk for writing
- Start with general talk, the children recalling what they did in the playground with the different toys. Use the photos to stimulate their discussion.
- Look at the three scooter photos and talk about how the scooter moved, what made it go faster and how you keep safe. Ask the children to feedback ideas on each of these subjects in order to structure their talk and show them how to select specific information in preparation for writing.
- Introduce the idea of a new page for one of the books you have been reading.

> We haven't got a page about scooters in our book. Tomorrow shall we write a new page for the book about a scooter?

## Session 2
### Shared writing
TEACHER DEMONSTRATION

- Tell the children that they are going to write a new page for the book and look at the Big Book to remind them how the pages are set out.
- Point out: heading, introductory sentence, photos with captions, 'Did you know?' box.
- Show the layout for a new double-page spread that you have drawn out already.

> I'm going to start with the heading and the first sentence. Page 4 in the book is about cars, so the heading is Cars. Our page is about scooters, so I'm going to write Scooters for my heading. Why am I using a capital 'S'? Yes that's right, because it is a heading.

- Look at a few introductory sentences on different pages and point out that they tell us what the vehicle is used for.

> So I've got to say something about what a scooter is for. Well, children love playing on them, so I could say Scooters are for children to play on. How many words is that?

- Say each word of the sentence together and count the words.
- Write the next sentence. As you are writing, ask the children to listen carefully for the end of the first idea, and put their hands up when you have got to the end of the sentence. Read through what you have written with the children.
- Ask the children if it sounds like an information book.

## Session 3
### Shared writing
TEACHER SCRIBING

- Tell the children that they are going to continue writing our page about 'scooters', and writing the captions.
- Stick the photos into the three photo boxes on the page layout.
- Look at the first photo.

> Sam is pushing off with his foot on the ground to get the scooter going. Turn to your partner and create a sentence that we can use as a caption for this photo. … I'm going to use Meera's idea because she started her sentence with A scooter is … and that's how the other captions started in the book, A tanker is …, A car is …. Meera's was a good sentence: A scooter is moved by pushing with your foot. I'm going to write that now in the right place on the page.

- Write the sentence in the first caption box. Ask for contributions for a second sentence for this photo.
- Point to the second photo. Ask for ideas for this photo. A child might say It went whizzing down the hill like a rocket. Model back using 'information-book language', eg Scooters go faster down a hill, explaining that you don't use descriptive language in the same way as you would in stories or poems.

> The last word is hill. Segment the phonemes. How many are there? We heard three phonemes. Now we will spell the word h-i-ll. What do you notice? There are four letters but only three phonemes. The final phoneme has two letters but only one sound. Let's reread the whole caption together Scooters go faster down a hill.

## Session 4

### Shared writing

SUPPORTED COMPOSITION

- Hand out dry-wipe boards and pens (one between two).
- Ask the children to write two more sentences for this photo. Reiterate the importance of discussing the sentence before they write it, and reading it as they write it to check they haven't missed any words out. Stop the children after most have written their first sentences to discuss what they have written, to pick up on particularly good examples and iron out any misconceptions, such as sentences which do not relate to the topic or non-sentences.

### Independent work

Ask the children to write two or three more sentences for the third photo. Ask some children to write on OHTs so that their sentences might be looked at by the whole class in the plenary session.

### Plenary

Look at three groups' sentences and discuss their merits with the class.

She havl to wer hrr helmt
beoss you mit hrt yor scf. She yost hrr foot
to poosh.

## Session 5
### Talk for writing

- Look back at the page written so far and explain that to complete the two pages they need something in the 'Did you know?' box. Look at the boxes in the book to see what sort of ideas they have. Read a few and draw out the idea that they are about interesting or unusual facts, eg **Some trains hang under the track.**

- Ask them to talk to their partners about an interesting fact about a scooter. Talk could be supported by giving out pictures from catalogues or newspapers of different types of scooter, and people using scooters. The children could talk about their own scooters, the cost of scooters, funny pictures of people on scooters, business people on scooters.

- Tell the children that they are going to write their own 'Did you know?' box. Show the format and explain where the sentence will go. Explain that they are going to write one sentence, using one idea, and draw a picture. Ask them to turn to their partners and help each other choose the best idea and make sure t's a sentence.

### Independent work

Children write the sentence and draw an illustration using their ideas from the paired talk.

GUIDED WRITING

Work with one group as they write their 'Did you know?' boxes. Prompt for use of capital letter and full stop and use the term 'sentence' when talking about their captions. Help the children to rephrase their writing so that it sounds more like information, eg instead of **I've got a silver scooter** they could write **Most new scooters are silver.**

### Plenary

- Once the independent writing is complete, collect together all the 'Did you know?' boxes that the children have written.

> We're going to put these in our book after our scooter pages. What are we looking for in this piece of writing? We want an interesting or unusual fact about scooters written in one sentence.

- Read a couple of examples and check that this is what they have done.
- Affix the 'scooter' pages and the 'Did you know' pages to the back of the book.

## What next?

The additional pages that you have added could be listed in the contents and the word scooter added to the index (use Post-it notes). A more able group could be given a new page to write for themselves, eg about roller blades or skateboards. Give children the format for a double-page spread. Ask them to write the heading and introductory sentence, draw pictures, write captions and a 'Did you know?' box.

# UNIT 8
# Y1 Term 3: The Magic Box

**Target:** To compose poetic sentences and extend vocabulary
**Pupil target:** I can make up a sentence for a poem using my own words and ideas.
**Outcome:** A new poem inspired by children's own experiences, using the structure of a poem read together
**Range:** Poetry

## OBJECTIVES

**T15**   to use poems or parts of poems as models for own writing, e.g. by substituting words or elaborating on the text;

**T16**   to compose own poetic sentences, using repetitive patterns, carefully selected sentences and imagery;

**W8**   new words from reading and shared experiences, and to make collections of personal interest or significant words and words linked to particular topics;

## Purpose and context

- Starting points could arise from circle time, drama or storytelling – activities to introduce the idea of memories and explore it together, eg in circle time, the children close their eyes and think about a happy thing, a sad thing or an angry thing that they remember. They can choose one of these things to talk about to the rest of the group.
- Help them to record this memory – is there one object, colour, or sound that helps them to remember this? Make notes of some ideas.
- Introduce the idea of a memory box – 'How could you capture these memories for ever?' Choose things to put in an imaginary box.
- Read *Wilfred Gordon Macdonald Partridge* by Mem Fox. Talk about the link between the objects and the memories they spark for Miss Nancy.
- Read the poem 'The Magic Box' by Kit Wright – probably many times over a period of time. Encourage the children to respond to the poem. Which things made them laugh? Which things did they like the best? Do any of the sentences give them a picture in their minds? Go back and look at the words used to create the image. Spend time talking about what is in the box. Talk about the way that 'pictures' in the poem may make you think about different feelings.
- Imagine the box itself. What would it look like? The children could draw or make their impression of the magic box.

## Session 1
### Talk for writing

- Play a game imagining each child has a magic box to put a memory into. Take it in turns to make up a sentence, In my box I will put ... and think of something that will remind them of a particular event, time, person, place (linked to the ideas they have come up with previously).
- Introduce the idea of writing sentences for a new poem using these ideas.
- Demonstrate how words can be chosen to extend the sentence, making it more detailed, helping to create a picture in their heads.

> Jasmin remembered when
> she played with bubbles in the bath and made everybody laugh.
> She could put a bubble in the magic box to help her remember. How
> could we describe that bubble?

- The children could talk about words to describe a soap bubble, what it looks like, how it moves, etc. List these words.

## Session 2
### Shared writing
TEACHER DEMONSTRATION

- Write up the sentence stem In my box I will put … and explain that you will use some of the ideas to complete the sentence for the poem. Draw attention to the use of the capital I for the personal pronoun as well as the capital letter at the beginning of the sentence.

> I don't want to just say In my box I will put a
> bubble. I am going to use some of your ideas so that you can see
> a picture of the bubble in your head when you read the poem. We said that
> a bubble is round, it floats, it has rainbow colours in it.
> I'm going to write a round, floating bubble. I think I could add a bit
> more to that, I'll add full of rainbow colours. Let's read
> that sentence together.

TEACHER SCRIBING

- Take another idea from the children to use for the next sentence. Change the mood by asking for a sad memory this time.
- Give time for the children to talk in pairs, thinking of words to describe the next item. Take some suggestions. Reinforce the idea of adding more detail to the basic idea in the sentence by looking back at the first sentence and how more detail was added. Emphasise the importance of saying the sentence aloud and trying out different words to see what sounds best.

> We've
> thought of something that will
> make us laugh so shall we take a sad memory
> next? Joshua suggested a plaster, to remind him of
> when he hurt his knee in the playground. A plaster is pink,
> sticky, sometimes it pinches … We could try out a sentence like
> this In my box I will put a sticky plaster for a cut knee. Does
> that sound alright? Shall we change any of the words? It might
> sound better if we changed sticky to pink, and added the
> word poor before cut. Now we've got In my box I will
> put a pink plaster for a poor cut knee.

- Talk with the children about the best choice of words, demonstrating how words can be added, deleted or changed. Keep reading the sentence through with the children until you are happy with it.

## Session 3
### Talk for writing and supported composition

- Reread the poetic sentences written in the previous session. Remind children of the way that the words represent a memory, and the way that more detail was added by choosing extra words to add to the sentence.

- Sit in a circle. Each child imagines their box and one or two memories they want to keep in it. Give children time to think about their own ideas, and then go round the circle with each child describing one thing. Give out sheets (on clipboards) with the sentence stem *In my box I will put a …* already written twice. Children talk with their partner and then each take a turn to add their own idea to complete the sentence stem.

- As they write, support and prompt with questions, eg 'What does it look like? What does it do?' Encourage the children to add further description, rereading their sentence with their partner and changing it until they are happy with the completed sentence.

- Go round circle with each child reading out their own completed sentence. Talk about the effect of reading out all the sentences – they have created a poem together. The repetition of *In my box I will put …* is like the Kit Wright poem.

- These ideas could be collected together for a class book – each page with its own illustration by the child who wrote the sentence.

## Independent work

The children can work independently to write their own sentences for the poem. They start with the sentence written in supported composition and then think of more things for their box, using the repeated sentence stem each time.

### GUIDED WRITING

Look at the verse in the Kit Wright poem which describes what the box looks like. The children can think about their own picture of the magic box and discuss this briefly. They then each write one sentence using the stem The magic box is … and choose words to describe the box. Challenge the children to use imaginative vocabulary, and to think of ways to improve their own sentence. Put the sentences together to make a new verse for the class poem, and discuss the order of the sentences. Which one should go first? Talk together about the effect of changing the order of the sentences.

### OTHER INDEPENDENT WORK

Children have a 'magic box' to look at. They choose one item from inside and write their own description to complete the sentence stem In my box I will put ….

## Plenary

- Bring together the different parts of the poem that have been written together, including the new verse describing the box. Read the whole poem together. Are they happy with the order of the lines? Should these be changed around, eg alternating happy and sad memories, or grouping together similar ideas?
- Can children pick out new vocabulary used in their writing? Why have particular words been chosen? What was the effect of using a particular word?
- Compare the new poem to the original. What are the similarities and differences? When you hear the new poem, can you imagine 'pictures' in your mind?

## What next?

- Read other poems to spark children's own imaginative ideas. Make a class anthology of poems that you have read frequently together, and make a taped version for children to listen to.
- Use another sentence stem as a starting point, eg At the end of the rainbow I saw …, Icicles are like … and build class poems with repetitive lines. Emphasise the choice of effective language.
- Look for examples of simple imagery used in a poem or story, eg quick as a cricket. Play games making up new similes.

# UNIT 9

# Y1 Term 3: The Day the Fire Engine Came to School

**Target:** To write a simple factual recount using a series of sentences linked by temporal connectives

**Pupil target:** I can write some sentences to recount something that has happened.          My sentences are in the right order.

**Outcome:** Recount using temporal connectives, about a visit (when the fire engine came to school)

**Range:** Recounts of visits, events

## OBJECTIVES

**T20**    to write simple recounts linked to topics of interest/study or to personal experiences, using the language of texts read as models for own writing. Make class/group books; (**T22** to write own questions prior to reading for information and to record answers.)

**T18**    … to begin to recognise generic structure of recounts, e.g. ordered sequence of events, use of words like first, next, after, when;

**S5**    other common uses of capitalisation … headings, titles …;

**S6**    … to reinforce knowledge of the term *sentence* …;

**S7**    to add question marks to questions;

**W8**    new words from … shared experiences …;

**W6**    to learn spellings of verbs with 'ed' endings …;

**Geography Scheme of work**

If the class has recently completed a visit to a place of interest, this unit could provide a very useful link 'Our Trip to …'.

## Purpose and context

- A visit by the fire engine to school is used to generate a purpose for writing. During the visit take lots of photos including, eg the fire engine arriving, the fire engine with ladder, child climbing ladder.
- You will already have read factual recounts with the class and identified temporal connectives such as first, next, last week. These can be made into a poster and displayed on the wall, so that you can refer to them when you are writing.

## Session 1
### Talk for writing

- Model asking questions to recall the event. 'Do you remember the special thing that happened the other day?' Ask general questions to recall what happened – things they saw, eg 'What came to our school? How many fire fighters were there?'
- Ask the children to turn to their partners and ask them a question about the visit. Share examples of questions. Structure and sort questions by providing model: Who? Where? When? What? Remodel the questions using key question words.

- Give each pair of children a card with a question word on it. Ask them to make a question using this word at the beginning to find out what happened. Give the children time to talk and compose their questions together.
- Take examples of each type of question from the children and select one of each to write up. As you write, remind the children of the use of question marks.

> I've finished writing the question Who came to our school last week but what do I need to put at the end? I don't want a full stop because I've written a question. I need to put a question mark instead.

- Go through each question and write a brief answer that can be used in the next session.
- Write up lists of new words (fire engine, fire fighters, ladder, hose) to use in the next session.

## Session 2
### Shared writing
TEACHER DEMONSTRATION

- Look back at the questions and answers from Session 1 to revise work on the visit. Explain that the class is going to make a wall display of the visit. Show photos taken on the day of visit. Explain that the children will be writing a recount of what happened so that visitors can read about the visit. Refer back to the collection of useful words and answers to questions.
- Sequence the photos in the correct order. Talk with the children about what happened first, next, finally.
- Take the photo that you will use first and tell the children that you are going to write about what happened in the photo. Write on piece of card so that the caption can be used on the display.

> Now, what happened in this photo? The fire engine arrives at school. Now, how shall I say that? It's not happening now, so I need to say arrived. The fire engine arrived at school. Now, I want to say something about what it looked like. Let's look at the questions and answers from the first session. Here's an answer about what the fire engine looked like – the fire engine was red and big, and had a long ladder on the top. I'm going to write that next. Now, I need a capital 'T' for The. Now, fire engine – I need to look at our collection of new words we made after the visit, to see how to spell them. Oh yes, f-i-r-e e-n-g-i-n-e (say letters).

- Write two sentences using the word list for ladder. Reread the sentences. Ask the children to close their eyes and listen while you read the sentences, and to put up their hands when they think you have got to the end of each sentence. Pin up the photo of the fire engine and the two sentences.
- Take ideas and decide on an appropriate title. Write The day a fire engine visited our school (remember to point out the -ed ending).

> What have we done today?
> We have used the answers from our questions to help us write about the visit. We have written two sentences with two ideas and put them up with the photo. Then we wrote the heading for the display in capital letters. Tomorrow, you are going to help write the other sentences for the display.

## Session 3
### Shared writing
TEACHER SCRIBING AND SUPPORTED COMPOSITION

● Use the example of the sentences written in Session 2 to write further sentences for other photos. Point to another photo and ask the children to turn to a partner and compose a sentence. Remind them to use the past tense. Take ideas. Write, eg The fire fighter showed us the long ladder

> Now, I want to add something more because he let some of you climb a little way up the ladder. Look at the list of connectives we wrote – next, then, first, after. Which word would we start our new sentence with? We want to say something about you climbing the ladder, and we want to use one of our special words. Turn to your partner and compose the next sentence using the past tense and a connective. … I'm going to use Joshua's idea because he used an -ed ending and one of the words from our list.

● Write, eg Then Jack and Maisy climbed up the ladder. Refer to the word list to support spelling ladder. Pin up the photo and the two new sentences on the display.

● Look together at the next photo, eg children trying on helmets and coats. Ask what happened next. Ask the children in pairs (able with less able) to think of the next sentence, using an appropriate connective from the list to start their sentence. They then write this on their dry-wipe boards. Remind them to use ideas from the answers to the questions, and to use the word list to help with spellings. Ask them to check for -ed endings and use of appropriate connectives, eg Next we tried on the fire fighters' helmets. Zac tried on one of the coats.

### Independent work
The children can work in groups using one photo per group, but each writing independently. They are aiming for two sentences, the correct verb ending (-ed), appropriate connective and words from the new vocabulary list.

## Plenary

- Pin up the completed sentences with the photo. Revisit the work done throughout the week. Talk about how you arrived at the wall display. Revisit the key objectives.
- Remind children that if they have to write about something that happened, a visit or an event, they should use the example on their wall display to help them. The wall display should by now have photos and sentences recounting the visit. There could also be adjacent a word list, a list of verbs with -ed endings and a list of temporal connectives. (These features could be highlighted in some way on the display.)

## What next?

Ask the children to write a simple recount of a further school visit, eg to a library or a church, using criteria for writing a recount. The expectation is that children will use: past tense, -ed verb endings, temporal connectives, sequenced ideas, sentences with correct punctuation, words from a collected list (eg church, pulpit, altar, pews, aisle).

---

CLASS NOTICEBOARD

*The Day the Fire Engine Visited Our School*

| We used special words: | We collected past tense verbs: |
| --- | --- |
| next | arrived |
| then | helped |
| after | climbed |

# Developing the concept of a sentence

## OBJECTIVES

**Y1 Term 1**

**S4–S8** to write captions and simple sentences, and to re-read, recognising whether or not they make sense, e.g. missing words, wrong word order; to recognise full stops and capital letters when reading, and name them correctly; to begin using the term sentence to identify sentences in text; that a line of writing is not necessarily the same as a sentence; to begin using full stops to demarcate sentences;

**Y1 Term 2**

**S4–S6** to recognise full stops and capital letters when reading and understand how they affect the way a passage is read; to continue demarcating sentences in writing, ending a sentence with a full stop; to use the term sentence appropriately to identify sentences in text, ie those demarcated by capital letters and full stops;

**Y1 Term 3**

**S6** through reading and writing reinforce knowledge of term *sentence* from previous terms;

**Text level objectives which extend children's understanding or require children to write sentences:**
**Y1 Term 1:** T3, T9, T10, T11, T14, T15, T16;
**Y1 Term 2:** T4, T15, T16, T23, T25
**Y1 Term 3:** T13, T14, T20, T21

## Principles and explanation

● When children arrive in Year 1, many are able to spell words sufficiently well for others to read them. The concept of a word is becoming established so that they can break the speech or thought stream into words for writing down, although they may still have to be reminded to put a space between words.

● Breaking the speech/thought stream into discrete sentences is a skill which is still developing in Year 1. Continue the two-fold approach started in Reception:
  – sentence level: model the writing of captions, labels and two or three sentences to describe an event and expect children to do this for themselves;
  – text level: encourage children to write recounts and narratives themselves (using their developing spelling ability) and also by scribing for them.

● By the end of Year 1 children can write a simple narrative or recount with some connectives other than and then which indicates that they are beginning to break the thought/speech stream into sentences, even if the punctuation is not always accurate.

● At sentence level this is achieved by showing children how to punctuate the single sentences they write and then expecting them to write two sentences and correctly demarcate them, and so on. At text level, continued exposure to texts and writing demonstration by the teacher enables children to imitate literary structures and to start to form their ideas into sentences.

- Explaining what a sentence is to young children is particularly difficult. They are taught that, in books, a sentence starts with a capital letter and ends with a full stop and that they should observe this practice when they write. But how to recognise when you have written a sentence is another matter. Some children are helped by being told that a sentence makes sense on its own and is complete; that it consists of an idea. Children should point out the sentences in shared reading and should have plenty of opportunities to experiment with constructing sentences orally as well as writing them.

- Some books arrange sentences so that they fit a single line of text. This is misleading as children may deduce that a sentence is a line of print. In shared reading, read some books where this has not been engineered and when you write on the board, allow some sentences to over-run a line.

- Children should be reminded to think of the whole sentence (an idea) and say it aloud before they start to write. However, young children still sometimes miss out a word as their pace of writing is slow. Rereading and checking should become a habit. Children who continually omit words should be encouraged to point to each word as they reread. This makes omissions more obvious.

- Just as in Reception, the word/sentence level time in the Literacy Hour in Year 1 Term 1 will be used for phonics. Work on sentences should take place during shared text work.

## Quick, whole class activities to develop the concept of a sentence

- With the help of the children, write captions for a display in the classroom, eg **Plastic bottles can be recycled. Never leave taps running. Save your newspapers**. Use a square piece of paper for the captions so that the sentence takes up two lines. Emphasise the capital letter and the full stop.

- When the children have really got to know a book well, write some of the sentences out on card, and cut each sentence into two parts. Give the cards out to pairs of children and give them a few moments to read them together, checking with you or other children for any words they are stuck on. Now tell the children to find the pair of children with the other half of their sentence and to go and sit down with them. Ask them to be sure the sentence makes sense and that it has a capital letter at the beginning and a full stop at the end. Choose two or three groups of children to read their sentences out.

- Copy a page of text from a book not well known by the children. Leave occasional verbs, pronouns or prepositions out, but don't leave a space. Read through with the children sentence by sentence, stopping where they think there's a word missed out. The children could write possible words on their dry-wipe boards and then you could discuss the best of the alternatives.
- Provide sentences and non-sentences on strips. A child takes a strip and holds it up and the children read it and decide whether it goes on the sentences or non-sentences pile, eg:

The was playing.
The boy was playing.
The boy the ball.
The boy playing.
Was playing by himself.
Playing in the sand.
The boy was playing by himself.

- Read a sentence aloud. The children should repeat it and count the number of words.
- When writing sentences, rehearse the sentence and count the number of words. After writing, double check.
- Use an acetate overlay (or other text marking device such as highlighter tape) to identify and underline sentences in a text.
- Work on a familiar tale, such as *The Gingerbread Man*, and write down a shared version, leaving out all the full stops. Reread at horse racing pace! Then give out small lumps of Blu-tak and reread so the children can hear where full stops should go. Pupils can insert Blu-tak 'full stops'.
- Provide incomplete sentences on strips – first part, eg The little cat, The big dog, and second part, eg sat in a tree. ran to me. The children match the halves to create sentences.
- Provide partial sentences written on a sheet for children to complete. Read a few chosen sentences. 'Are they complete? Do they sound right? Do they make sense? Do they need finishing?'
- Write a short story on the computer in which the capital letters and full stops have been placed incorrectly. Read this – does it sound right? Alter by rereading and listening to hear when the sentence is complete, eg:

The cat was sitting in the.
Sun he was getting very.
Hot just then an ice-cream.
Van came past the cat.
Jumped up he ran to get.
An ice-cream

- Rainbow sentences:
  - Choose a passage (without direct speech) from a familiar text. Ask the children to read it aloud so you can scribe it, using a different colour for each sentence – rainbow sentences. (Make sure some of your sentences don't end at the end of the line.) Point out how the colour shows the sentence boundaries.
  - Give the children two coloured pens and a dry-wipe board. Help them to construct a sentence which they write in one colour followed by another sentence in the other colour and so on.

- Construct two sentences with the children to label a display, as a reminder to the class of some pending event such as the school fete, Mikhail's dentist appointment at half past one, etc. Try to vary the openings (and therefore the construction) of sentences, eg Mikhail's appointment is at … could become At 1.30, Mikhail ….

- Play a quickfire game where you say a sentence or not a sentence – something that is complete or not – and the children put their thumbs up or down, depending on whether the idea runs as a complete sentence or not. This can be used too when rereading children's work or examples written by the teacher to check if sentences have been demarcated.

- Reread favourite stories encouraging the children to join in until they are known by heart. Tell the stories round a circle or as call and response with you saying one sentence and the children saying the next. Occasionally make deliberate mistakes by saying something that is not a sentence! Constant retelling helps to embed sentence patterns in children's language that they can then use in their own writing.

- Compose stories in a circle, each child inventing the next complete sentence.

- During shared or guided reading, ask the children to read round the group, one sentence each.

- During shared reading, give one child a tennis ball, which she or he can bounce every time you reach a full stop. When the ball bounces, everyone else should say 'Capital letter!'

- Use magnetic words or words on card to create sentences. Discuss how words can be taken out to trim a sentence back and words added in to elaborate. Swap words over and discuss changes to meaning, eg The man ran down the lane. The man tiptoed down the lane.

## Shared writing

- Write poems with repetitive lines, eg:

At the end of the rainbow I saw …
In my magic box there is …
Icicles are like …

emphasising the sentence aspect as well as the search for ideas and effective language.

Look at the list of ideas that we have collected. We have said that the moon is like a banana, a smile, a horn, a bridge, and an eyebrow. Now I am going to start writing the poem. Who can help me with the first line? In pairs, put that first idea into a sentence. Jo, what have you got for a first sentence? The moon is like a banana. Good, I will write that up on the flip chart, and I mustn't forget to use a full stop. Let's reread that. I think that we could add to that. The moon is like a what banana? A shiny one? Ok, I'll include that word. So, now we have written, The moon is like a shiny banana.

Our next sentence is going to say that it is like a smile, what sort of a smile could we say – a white smile? That sounds good. In your pairs quickly make up a sentence with the words white smile. The moon is like a white smile up in the dark sky. Well, that sounds good. I like the way that you have added some extra words on the end, up in the dark sky.

I'm going to write my recount now about my family's trip to Bristol Zoo. I want to write in sentences and make no mistakes so I'm going to be very careful and reread my work. Now if I look at my plan I can see that I need to mention 'when', 'who', 'where' and 'what' in my first sentence. So – At the weekend my family went Bristol Zoo for the day. Now, what does that sound like? Listen carefully to see if it makes sense. Yes, that first sentence sounds odd. Can you see I have missed the word to out when I wrote it down?

- Use a sentence from a favourite story as a model for another version. For instance, with the book *Owl Babies* you might decide to begin Once upon a time there were three baby foxes ….
  (*Note: Owl Babies* is a 'written down' oral tale and 'A big branch for Sarah, a small branch for Percy, and an old bit of ivy for Bill.', though punctuated as such, is not a sentence.)
- Construct sentences with the children to describe an event, ie a simple narrative or recount. Use connectives between the sentences such as after that, later, next, etc.
- Imitate sentence structures and use them to create other similar sentences. For instance, take a sentence from *The Three Bears*, such as She tasted the first bowl of porridge but it was too hot. Now write a string of but sentences, eg He ran down the lane but it was too late. She talked to her dolls but it was not much fun.
- Take sentence structures that invite imaginative reinventions. For instance, in *Six Dinner Sid*, focus upon the part where we discover that Sid has different names and behaves in different ways for different neighbours:

  As Scaramouche Sid was gentle.
  As Barney Sid was bold.
  As Penelope Sid was purring.
  As Sally Sid was sly.
  As Patricia Sid was pretty.

- When children write, ask them to put a small tick at the bottom of the page as they write each sentence – or count the number of sentences and write the number down. Encourage them to be sentence spotters and writers.

# Capital letters and question marks

## OBJECTIVES

**Y1 Term 2**
**S7** to use capital letters for the personal pronoun 'I', for names and for the start of a sentence;
**Y1 Term 3**
**S5** other common uses of capitalisation, e.g. personal titles, headings, book titles, emphasis;

- Read a text written in the first person singular. Highlight all capital letters; discuss their use.
- Encourage the children to notice capital letters in other texts and to explain why they are used. Start a 'capitals' wall chart listing the reasons for using capital letters.
- Write a series of sentences about 'things we like', all using I like, eg I like to look at …, I like to hear the sound of ….
- Collect characters' names from texts and notice the use of capital letters.
- Organise children's names under alphabet headings. 'Which is the most popular capital letter to start a name in our class?'
- Occasionally omit capital letters when writing on the board – ask children to check your writing and refer to the 'capitals' wall chart – reread and correct.
- During shared writing, use capital letters for dramatic emphasis. Reread to demonstrate how this should be read. Find instances in texts. Create labels for display that use capitals for emphasis, eg Do not touch – Hammy BITES!
- Make a list of exclamations that can be used in story writing. Write in capitals to give emphasis, eg NO! HELP! RUN!
- Invent silly names for toys. List the names of pets and cuddly toys. Emphasise that names are important and so they have a capital letter.
- When writing down facts create simple lists of sentences under headings, using a capital letter for the heading.

## OBJECTIVES

**Y1 Term 2**
**T24** to write simple questions e.g. as part of an interactive display …;
**Y1 Term 3**
**S7** to add question marks to questions;
**Related text level objectives**
**Y1 Term 3:** T19, T22

- Compare how two sentences are spoken – a statement and a question, eg The old man sat on the donkey. Did the old man sit on the donkey?
- Read aloud and sort unpunctuated sentences written on strips of card into two piles – statements or questions.
- Where appropriate, throughout the week, focus upon asking questions – children and teacher – and modelling these in writing.
- Read simple texts and underline the question sentences. Circle question marks and prepare a reading of the questions.
- In pairs, one child reads a list of prepared questions – the other answers them. Concentrate on tone of voice.
- Use objects, posters or photographs to generate questions – use a five-fingered hand with Who?, Why?, Where?, When?, What?, to help ask questions. List other question sentence starters such as Did you …? Have you …? Can you …?

# Year 2

## Contents

| Unit and range | Term | Objectives | Links to curriculum | Page |
|---|---|---|---|---|
| **Unit 10**<br>Story with familiar setting | 1 | T10, T11<br>S2, S4 | Geography<br>Unit 3: An island home<br>Unit 4: The seaside | 88 |
| **Unit 11**<br>Instructions | 1 | T15, T16, T17, T18<br>S2, S4, S6<br>W7 | Science<br>Unit 2b: Plants and animals<br>in the local environment | 93 |
| **Unit 12**<br>Traditional stories/stories<br>from another culture | 2 | T13, T14<br>S3, S5, S9 | Geography<br>Unit 5: Where in the world<br>is Barnaby Bear? | 98 |
| **Unit 13**<br>Explanation; Glossary | 2 | T20, T21<br>S4, S7<br>W10 | Science<br>Unit 2E: Forces and movement | 104 |
| **Unit 14**<br>Texts with language play | 3 | T8, T9, T11<br>S2, S3<br>W10 | Music<br>Unit 2: Sounds interesting | 111 |
| **Unit 15**<br>Non-chronological report | 3 | T14, T19, T20, T21<br>S4, S5, S6 | Science<br>Unit 2A: Health and growth | 116 |

| Unit | Objectives | Page |
|---|---|---|
| **Unit A:** Y2 Term 1 | S2, T4, T11 | 132 |
| **Unit B:** Y2 Term 1 | S4; also: Y2 Term 2, S3, S4;<br>Y2 Term 3, S2 | 134 |
| **Unit C:** Y2 Term 1 | S5, S6 | 136 |
| **Unit D:** Y2 Term 2 | S5; also: Y2 Term 3, S3 | 138 |
| **Unit E:** Y2 Term 2 | S6 | 140 |
| **Unit F:** Y2 Term 2 | S7 | 141 |
| **Unit G:** Y2 Term 2 | S8; also: Y2 Term 3, S4 | 142 |
| **Unit H:** Y2 Term 2 | S9; also: Y2 Term 3, S5 | 144 |
| **Unit I:** Y2 Term 3 | S6, S7 | 148 |

# Introduction

By the beginning of Year 2 most children are becoming confident in writing for a range of purposes, including the ability to write a simple narrative, recount, non-chronological report and a set of instructions. They can orally 'rehearse' their sentences ahead of writing independently and show evidence of applying their knowledge of language and its structures gained from reading. Their independent writing demonstrates the ability to punctuate simple sentences and to use spelling strategies drawn from their growing phonic knowledge and skills, and sight vocabulary.

During Year 2 children will increasingly develop their ability to control their writing. They will learn more about the ways in which words and sentence structure can be extended, manipulated and linked in specific ways to suit context, purpose and audience and how the use of planning devices can support the development of more extended pieces of writing in which ideas can be linked coherently. The National Literacy Strategy *Framework for teaching* for Year 2 contains a range of text and sentence level objectives which are critical to this development of greater control over the writing process and the ability to use written forms which differ structurally from spoken language.

The six teaching units in this section are designed to provide exemplars of sessions which focus on some of these key objectives and targets for development in writing. The context for, and content of, children's writing is located within experience drawn from a range of sources – including work within other curriculum areas. An important aspect of every unit is the 'Talk for writing', designed to enable children to discuss orally the writing process and, under guidance and support from their teachers, to rehearse written language structures. Suggestions are also included for the development and use of simple planning devices and a variety of prompts to support children in drawing on prior knowledge, including that drawn from shared reading. The units demonstrate the role of the teacher in 'thinking aloud' as a writer who exhibits a number of strategies for independent writing and makes active use of scaffolds and prompts (see the section 'If I get stuck' in Part 1, page 19). The units also begin to introduce discrete sentence level activities within the overall context of the unit. The six units are followed by a 'Grammar for writing' section which describes a number of activities which can be undertaken in discrete sentence level teaching sessions and incorporated into the overall teaching sequence. Teachers of more able pupils will find it useful to consult the Year 3 section of *Grammar for writing* (DfEE 2000) for further material.

## Balance of whole class work in the Literacy Hour

The teaching units which follow have been written on the assumption that the balance of time has been allocated in Year 2 according to the principles suggested in the Introduction to this book (page 20). Some sessions will require spending up to 30 minutes on shared writing which covers both sentence and text level objectives. In planning your sequence of lessons, you will need to consider the way in which you need to apportion time to this type of session, as well as specific work at word or sentence level which is relevant to your overall objectives and targets for writing.

By the end of Year 2, in writing, most children will have learned to:

| | |
|---|---|
| Phonics and spelling | • Spell two-syllable words, eg **sometimes**, including some words with prefixes and suffixes.<br>• Spell the ends of regular past tense verbs with **-ed**.<br>• Spell all the words in Y1/Y2 list in Appendix List 1 in the NLS *Framework*. |
| Handwriting | • Use the four basic handwriting joins with confidence in independent writing. |
| Style: Language effects | • Consider and select from a range of word choices.<br>• Give detail to engage reader. |
| Style: Sentence construction | • Write simple sentences (using some prepositions).<br>• Begin to use conjunctions to write compound sentences.<br>• Use sentences from texts as models for writing. |
| Punctuation | • Punctuate some sentences in the course of writing, using capital letters, full stops and question marks.<br>• Begin to use commas in lists. |
| Purpose and organisation | • Write a recount or narrative in sentences using connectives that signal time, eg **then**, **next**, **meanwhile**, **later**.<br>• Begin to show some consistency in use of 1st or 3rd person and tense.<br>• Apply knowledge of story elements – such as settings, dialogue, characterisation, story language and structures so that own writing begins to 'sound like a story', with some consistency of genre and tense. Give sufficient detail to engage reader's interest.<br>• Begin to show some characteristics of chosen form, eg write non-chronological reports, based on structure of known texts, incorporating appropriate language to sequence and categorise ideas. |
| Process | • Write initial jottings, notes and ideas before writing.<br>• Rehearse sentences, and adapt and re-read during writing to identify where improvements might be made and to spot errors. |

From *Target statements for writing*
(NLS 2000); see disk accompanying this book

# UNIT 10
# Y2 Term 1: At the Seaside

**Target:** Write a recount or narrative in sentences using connectives that signal time
**Pupil target:** I can use connectives to link some of my sentences.
**Outcome:** Short story based at the seaside, making good use of connectives that signal time
**Range:** Stories with familiar settings

## OBJECTIVES

**T10**   to use story structure to write about (an) experience …;
**T11**   to use language of time … to structure a sequence of events …;
**S2**    to find examples … of words and phrases that link sentences …;
**S4**    to re-read own writing for sense and punctuation;

**QCA Geography Scheme of work**
Aspects of content and context for writing could be derived from either Unit 3: An island home or Unit 4: Going to the seaside, both of which involve children in identifying similarities and differences between their own local environment and a contrasting area.

## Purpose and context

Writing will arise from reading stories, recounts, etc. and discussing personal experiences. Possible starting points could be:

- reading one of Mairi Hedderwick's Katie Morag stories, eg *Katie Morag Delivers the Mail*;
- discussing how adventures at the seaside are different from those in towns and shopping centres. Have any of the children had an adventure at the seaside?
- experience drawn from work in geography on a contrasting locality – the seaside;
- the teacher telling her or his own 'At the seaside' story, which involves a clear sequence of events.

During shared reading sessions, help the children to build up a bank of connectives which occur across sentences. Some of these will link sentences to signal how events are sequenced, eg **meanwhile, then, next, afterwards, after a while, suddenly**. Others (conjunctions) can also be used to link ideas and actions *within* sentences, eg **after, before, when**. These could be made available to children either in the form of a wall display, or a filing system of alphabetically ordered connectives with examples to illustrate their use. Select texts for shared reading which provide clear models such as *Eat Up Gemma* by Sarah Hayes (Walker Books).

The emphasis of this writing unit is on the use of temporal connectives to link sentences in order to convey a sequence of events.

## Session 1
### Talk for writing
- Use a picture, eg from a commercial poster pack, a travel brochure, a postcard, a painting, showing people at the seaside as a starting point for inventing a class story.

● Find some children in the picture and give them names. Agree the beginning and development – but not the ending – of a story. Make sure that the children recognise that the beginning and the development must be related.

> Look at the children in the picture. They are paddling in the sea. What do you think might happen to them? … One of them could be stung by a jellyfish … or cut their foot … or see a pirate … or stub their toe on a treasure box sticking out of the sand … or catch sight of a mermaid behind these rocks … What do you think?

● Ask the children to suggest ideas, respond to them yourself and invite the rest of the children to consider them too, eg 'Do you really think sharks can swim in water that is this shallow?' Try to keep the children focused on the seaside theme and help them to develop their ideas to think about what could happen next, eg 'If you stubbed your toe on a treasure box, what would you do next? What do you think the child in the picture would do?'

● Model a way of jotting down planning on a three-stage diagram using arrows to connect successive events in the story. (You will need to keep a copy of the planning diagram to use at the beginning of the next session.) Tell the children that they can make a quick story plan to show the story so far. Ask what happened at the beginning of the story.

> The two children were at the seaside. I'm going to write that down Children at seaside. I don't need to write in sentences now because I'm just making notes to remind me about what I decided. Then we thought that one of the children would stub their toe on a treasure chest, so I'll write Jamil stubbed toe on treasure chest. Is this a good sentence? No, but it doesn't need to be because I'm only writing notes. We decided that the children would dig up the treasure chest and find a pirate treasure inside it. How should I write that on my plan? … Do I need to use sentences? Now I can draw arrows between my notes to show the order they happened in.

● Talk about possible endings. Encourage the children to develop their own ideas, but continue to emphasise that the ending must follow on logically from the rest of the story. Ask them how they think the story should end. Suggest that it could end in lots of different ways and ask them to talk to a friend and decide how they think this story would end.

## Session 2
### Shared writing
TEACHER DEMONSTRATION

● Display the planning diagram prepared in the previous session. Referring to this, demonstrate how to use the planning notes to develop the story.

> Now what was the first note ... Children at seaside. That's to remind me that the setting of our story is the seaside. The setting is the place where the story begins. I could make that note into a sentence by saying One day, Jamil and his sister went to the seaside. but I don't think that's a very interesting start to the story. It's good if you can start a story with some action because that makes the readers want to know more and then they keep on reading to find out what's going to happen.

> Let me think ... what other notes have I made? ... Oh yes, Jamil stubbed toe on treasure chest. I think I'll begin with that because it sounds exciting – I need to make it into a proper sentence and I need to show that he's at the seaside, but I don't think I'll tell our readers yet that it was a treasure chest: I'm going to write: Jamil was paddling in the sea. Suddenly he stubbed his toe on something in the sand.

- Ask the children to talk in pairs and then tell you about how the reader would know from this that Jamil was at the seaside and how these opening sentences might make the reader want to read on.
- Now explain that you are going to continue to write the beginning of the story and will use the planning diagram to remind you of what they decided was going to happen. As you write, make your thought processes explicit about the way you are developing the notes into sentences and the decisions that have to be made.

> I need to use a capital letter because it's the beginning of a sentence. ... I didn't have a verb in my notes, so I'll need to put one in. ... I need a good word to help me show how Jamil felt. ... I need to remember the full stop at the end of my sentence.

- After you have written about three or four sentences, reread them reflecting aloud on whether these short sentences have shown how the events in the story are sequenced. Discuss with the children how some of the sentences could be started in order to show this. Remind the children of the work they have already done on connectives and refer them to the class connectives bank.
- Reread your sentences again, drawing the children's attention to whether the story has followed the sequence set out in the plan.

TEACHER SCRIBING

- Take suggestions from the children as to what they had agreed happened next, and let them hear your evaluations of them. Help the children to recognise that their suggestions should be linked as closely as possible to your original story plan.

- Take one of the children's ideas and ask the others to help to recast the idea as a sentence. Once you have agreed a sentence content and structure, ask for the children's ideas for a connective, eg 'Can anyone suggest a word I could use to introduce this sentence?'
- As you scribe the sentence, take a few opportunities to ask different children to spell high frequency words, or regular, monosyllabic words which contain long vowel sounds. Continue to develop the story in this way until you have told it up to the point at which you stopped planning earlier. After you have added each sentence, remind the children to read it aloud and to make sure that it makes sense and is correctly punctuated.
- Before you finish, reread the whole story so far, and check for any possible improvements.

## Independent work
- Begin to make a planning diagram like the one used earlier to tell a personal story.
- Work in pairs, reading books set at the seaside from the class library. Discuss how successive events in the story are related. Which sequencing words are used in the story?
- Work in pairs, looking at pictures of the seaside. Write short descriptions of the seaside as a setting, focusing on spelling.

## Plenary
- Ask the children to retell the 'story so far' of your shared story. Each child can only say one sentence. The next child must begin their sentence with a connective, eg Then ..., After a while ..., Next ....
- Discuss whether all the sequencing connectives are necessary, or whether some could be cut.

## Session 3
## Talk for writing
*Exploring the use of connectives to sequence events*

- Prepare strips of card showing sentences such as these:

| |
|---|
| After breakfast Sarah and Jamil went down to the beach. |
| First they paddled in the sea. |
| Suddenly Jamil stubbed his toe. |
| After that they found the treasure chest. |
| Then it was time for lunch. |
| Afterwards they went back to the beach to swim. |
| After a while they got cold. |
| Before tea they made sandcastles. |
| Meanwhile Rover dug a deep hole. |

- Display the strips in an inappropriate order. Read them through, asking the children to think about whether the events in the story are in the right sequence and then involve them in discussing what is wrong. Ask children, in pairs, to decide which sentence should go first, etc. and help them to justify their decision. Build up the story into a logical sequence, then read it through together.

## Shared writing

### SUPPORTED COMPOSITION

Remind the children of the story you were telling together at the previous session. Show them the planning diagram you used for the last session, which stopped short of the ending.

● The children have dry-wipe boards (one between two). Ask each pair to discuss how the story is going to end and to write the next sentence of the story on their dry-wipe boards. Their sentence should start with a connective which shows how the sequence of events is moving on. Remind them to refer to the class connectives bank.

● Once each pair has written a sentence, ask some of them to read their sentences aloud. Ask them which connective they chose and whether it correctly described the order of events. Each pair should now try writing an alternative sentence. Both children should read both sentences aloud and evaluate them, trying to agree which is most effective.

● Ask various children to read aloud both sentences, to tell the class which one they decided on and why.

## Independent writing

All the children work by themselves to write the end of the story, beginning with their preferred sentence from their dry-wipe board. Before they begin to write, remind them:

● They are writing an ending for a story you have all begun. They can't change the story now – they just have to decide how it finishes. The planning notes are there to help.

● They should sometimes use connectives to show how the events in their stories are sequenced. Remind them of the class bank.

● As they finish each sentence, they should reread it for sense and punctuation.

● Once they have finished all their writing, they should reread it and check that it makes sense.

## Plenary

Give some children the chance to read their writing aloud. Ask the others to assess whether the reader has met the targets:

● Is it an ending for the story you all began together?

● Is the sequence of events clearly marked through the use of good connectives?

## What next?

● Let the children write a story, still based at the seaside, about their own experiences or let them invent another story.

● Give the children more opportunities to play oral games which explore how different connectives can be used to sequence events in stories, eg ask them to retell parts of a traditional tale or nursery story. Each successive person's turn should be signalled by the use of a connective.

● Help the children to find time sequencing connectives when they are reading.

# UNIT 11
# Y2 Term 1: Planting Beans

**Target:** Begin to show some characteristics of instructional texts, incorporating appropriate language
**Pupil target:** I can write instructions which have a goal at the beginning followed by a series of steps. I can use proper language for my instructions.
**Outcome:** A poster with instructions for planting a bean in a jar, accompanied by a labelled diagram
**Range:** Instructions

## OBJECTIVES

| | |
|---|---|
| **T15** | to write simple instructions …; |
| **T16** | to use models from reading to organise instructions sequentially …; |
| **T17** | to use diagrams in instructions …; |
| **T18** | to use appropriate register in writing instructions …. |
| **S2** | to find examples … of words and phrases that link sentences …; |
| **S4** | to re-read own writing for sense and punctuation; |
| **S6** | use a variety of simple organisational devices …; |
| **W7** | use word ending -ed …; |

**QCA Science scheme of work**
Content, context and purpose for writing could be drawn from Unit 2b: Plants and animals in the local environment.

This involves children in experimentation which enables them to observe and record the requirements of seeds in order to grow. The following of precise instructions for setting up the experiments is therefore critical.

## Purpose and context
Writing will arise from practical experience as part of the science curriculum. Before they attempt to complete this unit children will need to have:
- had experience of reading, and following, instructions. They will need to be aware of the key structural features of instruction texts;
- studied enough of the chosen science unit to know, for example, that plants produce seeds and that these seeds will grow into plants;
- compiled a list of key vocabulary.

## Session 1
This session is based on the children observing you as you plant a broad bean in a jar. You will need: a jar, a broad bean, blotting paper or cotton wool, water.

### Talk for writing
- Establish the activity in the context of the science unit.
- Explain to the children that you are going to plant a broad bean in the jar and that as you do this, they are going to have to think of ways of telling younger children how to do it.

- As you demonstrate each step (lining the jar with the cotton wool/blotting paper; putting the bean between the lining and the jar; adding water) ask the children to tell you what you have done.
- Demonstrate the jotting down of brief notes to support this.

> It's a useful idea to make notes to remind you what you've done. I've just rolled the blotting paper into a tube and put it inside the jar. Can you tell me how I could write this as a quick note? … Do I need to use full sentences? … I could just write Put paper in jar. That's enough to remind me of what I've done.

- When you have finished, discuss how the process would best be communicated to others. Can the children decide between a report, a recount or instructions? Help them to recognise that instructions are the most efficient way of telling someone how to do something.
- Tell the children that you need to look back at the notes you made when you were setting up the jar. Remind them that what you jotted down was only a note and that you now have to convert the notes into sentences. Ensure that the children refer to your notes while you rehearse together the sequence in which the instructions must be carried out.

## Session 2
### Shared writing
TEACHER DEMONSTRATION

> We are going to write a set of instructions to tell younger children how to plant a bean in a jar. We need to remember that at the beginning of a set of instructions we have to put the goal – what the instructions are for – and the things we need. So I'm going to write the title: How to plant a bean in a jar. The How to at the beginning of the title helps people to recognise that this is an instructional text.

> I now need to make a list of the things that I need. Since this is meant for younger children, perhaps instead of simply writing a list, I'll draw little pictures and label them. That will help the children to read the words.

- Before you write the first instruction, remind the children of the crucial language and layout conventions – possible use of numbers or words, such as first, second, next. No use of pronoun I or We but the use of a command verb: Roll the paper into a tube.
- When you have written the first instruction, reread it and check that it makes sense, that the language you have used is suitable and that spelling and punctuation are appropriate.

So my first instruction is First, roll the paper into a tube.
I need to check:

- Does it make sense? Yes. It clearly tells my reader what to do.
- Have I used I or we? No. Good, because when I'm giving someone instructions, I don't just tell them what I did.
- Have I used a sequencing word? Yes. I don't always need one, but they are useful in reminding the reader about the order to do things in.
- Have I used an action word, a command verb, near the beginning? Yes. Instructions nearly always have verbs either right at the beginning or after a sequencing word.
- Have I begun with a capital letter? Yes.
- Have I remembered to use a full stop at the end? Yes.
- I need to check my spelling. Can I see any mistakes?

## TEACHER SCRIBING

- Ask the children to remind you what you did next when you planted the bean. Can any of them recast the statement into an instruction? Let several children suggest alternatives, before you decide which one you are going to write. Explain to the children why you chose the suggestion you did, making sure that they understand how sentence structure is crucial.

I like this instruction because it begins with a sequencing word, then there is an action verb to tells me what to do. It doesn't use I or you, but it tells me clearly what I have to do next.

- Before you write, explain to the children that since you are beginning a new instruction, you will need to use a new line of text and begin your new instruction with a new number.
- As you scribe, take a few opportunities to ask different children to spell high frequency words, or regular, monosyllabic words which contain long vowel sounds.
- Write the agreed instruction (without punctuation) then reread it with the children, inviting them to suggest any amendments.
- Finish all the instructions in this way.

## Independent work

- With a teaching assistant, look at a variety of instructional texts from the class library, noticing different ways in which layout is used. Make a note of all the different organisational devices used, eg boxes, numbers, arrows, lines, etc.
- Draw a diagram of the bean in the jar and label it, using key words from the text.
- Make a 'You will need' list for someone who is preparing to plant a seed in a flowerpot of soil.
- Make a list of sequencing words you could use to introduce the next instruction.

## Plenary

- Ask the children who have looked at different organisational devices to report back to the class. They should be prepared to talk about the effectiveness of each and whether some are better than others in different contexts.
- Children who have considered sequencing words could suggest which ones they think would be useful and at which point in an instructional text.

## Session 3

### Talk for writing

- Write out a variation of the following recount text to describe how you planted your bean:

I rolled the blotting paper into a tube and put it inside the jar so it touched the edge of the jar all the way round. Then I pushed the bean down between the blotting paper and the jar. Finally, I poured water into the jar, making sure that the water didn't touch the bean.

- Use this as the basis for a Replace activity. The children should help you to edit out all the recount text language and replace them with instruction text language, eg **I made a tube …** should be replaced with **Make a tube …**.

> Let's start by underlining all the words we think are wrong for instructions. Can anybody find any words which shouldn't be in instruction texts? … **I** shouldn't be used in instructions. So let's underline all the **I**s.

> If we take **I** out of the first sentence what are we left with? **Rolled the blotting paper into a tube …** what's wrong with that as an instruction? … **Rolled** is in the past tense, we can tell that because it's got the past tense **-ed** verb ending. That's okay for writing a recount about something you've done. But which tense should we use for instructions? … The present tense. Does anyone know what we should change that to? **R … the blotting paper into a tube.** Can anyone see any other **-ed** past tense verb endings. Let's underline them and then we can think what we should change them into.

### Shared writing

SUPPORTED COMPOSITION

- The children have dry-wipe boards (one between two). Remind them of the sequence of events involved in planting the bean (as repeated in the Replace activity). Tell them that as part of a scientific experiment to see what happens if beans don't get any light, you are going to put the bean into a dark cupboard. Can they write an instruction to that effect?

- Ask different pairs of children to read out the instructions they have written. Let the other children comment on them, congratulating the writers on the appropriate features of their sentence structure.

## Independent work

Ask the children to make a poster giving instructions for planting a bean in a jar. Remind them to:

- refer to the list of key vocabulary;
- begin with a clear statement about what the instructions aim to achieve;
- include a 'You will need' box;
- think about the language of instructions;
- think about the layout, eg number instructions, starting each instruction on a new line.

If the children finish in time, let them draw a labelled diagram of the bean in the jar.

### GUIDED WRITING

A less able group will benefit if you all agree what each instruction should say before they write it. Work with a more able group to extend each instruction, adding more detail. Other groups will benefit from support with getting the language structures and spelling right.

## Plenary

- Let the children admire each other's posters and discuss what is good about them and what could be done to improve them. In addition to the language features, let the children think about presentation, use of colour, etc. which are important features of attractive posters.
- Discuss how the use of a labelled diagram adds to the information on a poster.

## What next?

- Let the children follow each other's instructions to plant their own beans. They could then use a diary or table to chart the weekly change in their bean's growth.
- The children can write instructions for other experiments or for classroom routines, perhaps for a new child or a supply teacher.
- As they encounter instruction texts in guided reading, remind the children of the language features.

# UNIT 12
# Y2 Term 2: Traditional Stories

**Target:** Apply knowledge of story elements, such as settings, dialogue, characterisation, story language and structures so that own writing begins to 'sound like a story', with some consistency of genre and tense

**Pupil target:** I can make decisions about the best words to use when I write and make the characters and places in my writing interesting.

**Outcome:** Own version of a traditional tale, based on a given scaffold showing sequence of events

**Range:** Traditional stories; stories from other cultures

## OBJECTIVES

| | |
|---|---|
| **T13** | to use story settings from reading …; |
| **T14** | to write character profiles …; |
| **S3** | to re-read own writing to check for grammatical sense and accuracy …; |
| **S5** | to use verb tenses with increasing accuracy in … writing …; |
| **S9** | to secure the use of simple sentences in own writing. |

**QCA Geography Scheme of work**
The content of and context for children's writing could be enhanced by connection to the Geography Unit 5: Where in the world is Barnaby Bear?, which involves the development of awareness of similarities and differences between other countries and their own.

## Purpose and context

● Writing will arise from reading a variety of traditional stories and stories from other cultures. The strongest links can be created when stories with very similar themes and structures from different cultures can be compared, eg the traditional English story of *Puss in Boots* together with *Jamil's Clever Cat* by Fiona French (Francis Lincoln 1999) which is a Bengali folk tale. (Sardul, the cleverest cat in town, learns that his master, Jamil the weaver, dreams about marrying the princess. Sardul resolves to help to make his master appear to be a rich prince and so takes his master's finest sari as a present for her. The princess and her father, the Rajah, are convinced that Jamil is wealthy and clever and a wedding is arranged. After the wedding Jamil takes his bride back to his house where she quickly learns to weave. Eventually, Jamil and his wife become very wealthy.)

● A class collection of story openings characteristic of traditional tales has been compiled from experience of shared and personal reading.

● Before you read the story, locate Bengal on a world map and establish what the children know about the people, climate, flora and fauna of that part of Asia.

## Session 1
### Talk for writing
*Drama to explore characterisation*
Before the children are able to develop character in their writing, great benefit will be derived from extending and exploring characters through drama activities.

- Read, or tell, the tale you want the children to focus on.
- Begin with a familiar activity to help children to think about the story and main characters. For example, using *Jamil's Clever Cat*, ask them to imitate the way the animals moved in the jungle.
- Ask the children which parts of the story they think tell you most about one of the main characters. 'When do we know what kind of a person Jamil is? Where is he at this time? What is he doing? How is he feeling?'
- Model hot-seating the character of Jamil. If possible you and a teaching assistant can begin to model the process. If you take on the hot-seat character of Jamil at the beginning of the book, the teaching assistant can begin to ask you questions about where you live, what you eat, what you like to do, etc. As soon as they feel confident, let the children join in, asking you questions.
- Let the children get into small groups to discuss questions they would like to ask Jamil at his wedding, then come back as a class so that they can pose the questions and hear you answer them in role. Encourage them to think about what Jamil's feelings are, his appearance, his worries, what he would like to do next, etc.
- The children could go back into their groups. Each group could elect a 'Jamil' to be hot-seated at the end of the book. You can circulate amongst the groups, helping them to phrase questions and helping the Jamils to try to answer them.

The children could compile and display a 'portrait gallery' of the characters in the story with 'key biographical' information. This could include each child thinking about the questions they would like to ask a hot-seated character together with the answers they think they would get.

## Session 2
### Talk for writing

Reread, or retell, the story you are focusing on. Before you have a class discussion, ask children to talk with friends about each of the issues. Each group should agree which character/setting/event they want to talk about and should establish what each child in the group is going to say. All the children should say something, however brief.

- **The characters:**

> Look at the portrait gallery we made after the drama session. Who are the most important characters in the story? What do we know about them? Which character do you like the most? Why?

- **The setting:**

> How many different places are mentioned in the story? How are the places different? Is what happens in any of places something that couldn't happen in any of the other places?

- **The significant events:**

> What is the story about? What happens? What is the sequence of events in the story?

## Shared writing

TEACHER DEMONSTRATION

This is based on a retelling of *Jamil's Clever Cat* but could easily be adapted for other stories.

● Begin to retell the story. Think aloud about what you plan to write.

> I'll begin my story with words that show the reader that it's a traditional story. I think I'll have a look at the list we made together because that will help me to think about how to begin … I could choose **Once upon a time …**; **Once in a far off land …**; **One day**…. I think I prefer … because …

● When you introduce the main character, start by giving a very factual account, eg **A man sat in his cottage, weaving**. Then, making obvious reference to the 'portraits' compiled earlier, model how you could edit the sentence.

> **A man** doesn't tell me very much. I need to introduce the man's name and the fact that he's a weaver, because both of these are important to the story. I think I'll change that to **Jamil, a weaver … sat in his cottage**. What else did we say about Jamil? Oh yes … I need to show that Jamil is a poor man and that his house is small and cold, so I'll change the sentence to **Once in a far off land, Jamil, a poor weaver sat in his small, cold house.**

● You will need to show the children how to use the symbol ∧ to indicate that they wish to add a word.
● Reread the sentence again, modelling the evaluation of each of the words, the spelling, punctuation, grammar, etc. Make a point of checking that the sentence is written in the past tense. Point out to the children that you have used your opening sentence to give the reader quite a lot of information about Jamil. Explain that in this one sentence, you have told the reader that:
  – this is a traditional tale, because we have used a traditional tale's opening;
  – the main character is called Jamil;
  – Jamil is a weaver;
  – he is poor;
  – he lives in a small, cold house.
  All of these things are important to the story, but we want to tell our reader about them as quickly as possible so we can get on with the action.
● Write another sentence, again referring to the 'portraits' and this time introducing Sardul. Again, show how you can improve the sentence from the fact that Sardul is a cat, to include information about how clever he is and what he does. Every time you change the sentence, reread it to keep a check on sense, grammar, punctuation, spelling, etc.

TEACHER SCRIBING

● Ask the children to suggest a simple sentence to tell what happens first in the story. Ask for ideas for the next sentence. Scribe a more factual account to begin with, then accept the children's ideas to add description and detail.

> We'll begin by writing Jamil told Sardul that he wanted to marry the princess. When do you think this happened? … Is it likely to be in the evening or the morning? … Was it warm or cold? … Let's put One cold, winter's morning at the beginning of the sentence. Why did Jamil want to marry the princess? … Does anyone remember? … We can add this information at the end of the sentence … Can anyone think of a good word we could use to join the two pieces of information?

● Continue to scribe the next few sentences, always beginning with a simpler statement and then exploring ways of adding interest by changing the vocabulary. If the new vocabulary the children suggest is phonically regular, ask them to have a go at spelling.
● As you write, occasionally leave out full stops, capital letters, etc. in the expectation that the children will identify the errors as you reread the sentences each time.

## Independent work

● More able children can compile charts, briefly comparing the main characters, setting, etc. of two stories: one traditional story and one from another culture.
● With a teaching assistant, develop a character sketch for one of the main characters. For example, it could take the form of a letter or a poster where the Rajah boasts about the qualities of his new son-in-law to be.
● Make a list of different ways of moving for each of the main characters. The children could use a simple thesaurus to help them to find words. Do they use different words for the characters moving in different settings?
● Compile a list of words to describe the Rajah's splendid palace. If you have covered work on antonyms (Word 11) children could be asked to identify how many of the antonyms of these words can be used to describe Jamil's house.

## Plenary

Ask the children to think about a character or setting from the story and to make up a sentence telling you about it, but without actually mentioning what it is. Can the other children guess which character or setting is being described?

## Session 3
### Talk for writing

● Write the following text (ideally on a dry-wipe board):

Jamil is in the forest. He can hear the sound of all the animals. Jamil walks towards the Rajah's palace. The animals hide in the garden. The Rajah hears all the animals coming. He thinks they are people.

- Use it as the basis for a 'replace activity'. Can the children recognise that this story is written in an inappropriate tense? Stories are usually written in the past tense. Ask which tense this is written in. Read the sentences one at a time and ask children to discuss in pairs which words are in the present tense. They can then highlight these and replace them with words in the past tense. Do the children know which words they are focusing on? Explain that all the words which are underlined are verbs and that verbs tell us what is happening in a sentence and whether it is in the present tense or the past tense.

## Session 4
### Shared writing
SUPPORTED COMPOSITION

- Involve the children in a discussion about the 'rules' for writing a sentence that they can remember. Write down some of their ideas.
- Introduce the children to a checklist which you have prepared to help them to construct their sentences appropriately:
  - Does my sentence make sense?
  - Have I given enough information?
  - Have I used interesting words?
  - Is my sentence written in the past tense?
  - Is my sentence punctuated properly?
  - Is my spelling as good as it can be?
- Tell the children that you are going to carry on with the writing of the story by thinking about the events which happened at the end. Show them the sentence you have written: **Jamil and the Princess got married**. Involve them in a discussion about whether this sentence meets the criteria in the checklist and whether it gives sufficient information. Scribe their suggestions, finally writing up the complete improved sentence.
- Distribute dry-wipe boards and pens (one between two). Ask the children to work in pairs to improve the next sentence in the story: **Jamil took the Princess to his home** in order to make it more informative and interesting. They might want to write what Jamil and the princess were thinking and feeling, what they were wearing or what Sardul was thinking. In your settings sentence you could describe the palace.
- Remind the children to reread each of their sentences when they have written them, using the checklist. Some children can then read aloud the sentences they have written whilst the class refer to the checklist. Model some 'peer' responses yourself before asking children to comment:

> When you are talking about what someone else has written, always start by saying something you like, and then say how it could be improved. So you could say I think you have used some very good words to describe the palace, but I think you could improve it by changing the word 'nice' for a better word.

## Independent work

● Prepare a very simple outline text for the children, leaving wide spaces between the lines, eg:

Jamil wanted to marry the princess.

Sardul, his cat, took a sari to the princess.

The Rajah said Jamil could marry the princess.

Jamil and the princess were married.

Jamil took the princess to his house.

The princess learned how to weave.

Jamil and the princess were rich.

● Ask the children to edit the text in the way you have been modelling. They can change words, add words, put in connectives, etc. – anything to help to improve the text. When they have finished, the children should write out the whole text and check it for sense, grammar, spelling, punctuation, etc.

### GUIDED WRITING

The teacher could work with one group to either support or extend their writing. With less able children, you may wish to focus first on adding connectives at the beginning of their sentences. More able children can be shown how to add in new sentences, giving additional details and commentary about the events in the story.

## Plenary

● Ask the children to read out their revised versions. Can any of the other children suggest an alternative word at any point which would strengthen the writing?
● Praise the children's attempts to improve the writing. Point out that they can improve their own writing in this way too.

## What next?

● Use the editing marks you have shown the children, eg ∧, to indicate where you think they should add more information in future pieces of writing.
● When the children read more traditional tales in guided reading, point out how language is used to create character and setting.
● Ask the children to retell a different tale, eg *Puss in Boots*. Can they use the same language features?

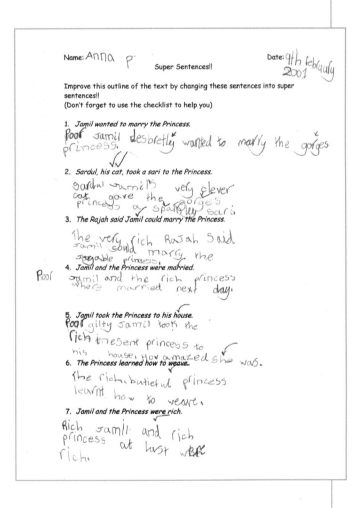

103

# UNIT 13
# Y2 Term 2: Explanations and Glossaries

**Target:** Begin to show some characteristics of explanatory texts based on structure of known texts, incorporating appropriate language to sequence and categorise ideas

**Pupil target:** I can write definitions to make a glossary. I can explain something using diagrams and explanatory texts.

**Outcome:** The beginning of a booklet of explanations, eg 'Speeding things up'. The booklet should include a cover, contents page, and glossary, as well as explanations and diagrams

**Range:** (i) Dictionaries, glossaries and other alphabetically ordered texts; (ii) explanations

## OBJECTIVES

| | |
|---|---|
| **T20** | to make class dictionaries or glossaries of special interest words, giving explanations and definitions …; |
| **T21** | to produce simple flow charts or diagrams that explain a process. |
| **S4** | to be aware of the need for grammatical agreement …; |
| **S7** | to investigate and recognise a range of other ways of presenting text …; |
| **W10** | new words from reading linked to particular topics …; |

**QCA Science scheme of work**
Content and context for writing could be derived from Unit 2E: Forces and movement, which requires children to explain how to make familiar objects move faster and slower.

## Purpose and context
Writing could occur in the context of simple science experiments to investigate how to make simple objects move faster or slower. Pupils should be familiar with conducting simple experiments and discussing their observations.

● Before they undertake the writing activity, children will need to have experience of:
  – looking up words in dictionaries and glossaries, using alphabetical order;
  – reading definitions and explanations.
● Writing simple reports – explanations require many of the same language structures as reports, but explanations are an extension of report texts, in that they explain phenomena, rather than simply describing them. In order that they can write satisfactory explanations, children need to be able to:
  – recognise how different bits of information relate to each other and organise a text to show these relationships;
  – use cause and effect connectives to link ideas within a sentence;
  – summarise the information in a text;
  – compile class lists of technical vocabulary related to their science experiments from shared reading of explanatory text, discussing the use of conjunctions which relate to cause and effect, eg **because**, **so**.

Section 2 in Part 3 of this book contains a summary of the features of non-fiction text types.

## Session 1
### Talk for writing

This session is based on an experiment to investigate how a toy car can be made to go faster down a ramp. (Most of the ideas can be adapted, if you prefer to base the writing on a different source.) The experiment should have been carried out in a previous science lesson, so that children have already investigated how the height of a ramp affects the speed of the car. It is helpful if you have the ramp and car available to act as a reminder to the children.

● Put the ramp flat on the floor and place the toy car on it. Ask a series of questions:

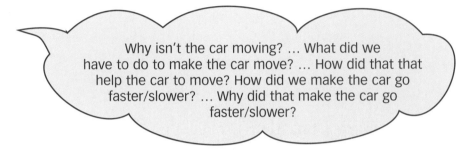

Why isn't the car moving? … What did we have to do to make the car move? … How did that that help the car to move? How did we make the car go faster/slower? … Why did that make the car go faster/slower?

● As you ask each of the questions, help the children to develop their ideas beyond a simple description, to include an explanation of why the action would affect the speed of the car. Each time one of the children has finished their explanation, it is helpful if you summarise what has been said, eg 'So, the car travels faster if I raise the ramp because it is going down a steeper slope.' In your summaries, draw attention to the use of cause and effect conjunctions like **because** which are very useful in explanatory texts.

### Shared writing

Tell the children that you are going to work together to explain that cars travel faster if the height of the ramp is raised, and that you will need to use both diagrams and writing in your explanations.

TEACHER DEMONSTRATION

● Display two simple, unlabelled diagrams, telling the children that these show the heights of the different ramps, and the reason the ramps are different heights (in this case two more bricks). Label the diagrams talking aloud about what you are doing.

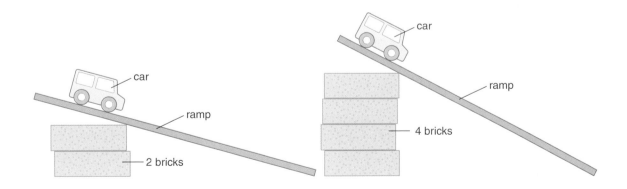

● Under the first diagram, write the beginning of a simple explanation of what you observed. As you write, talk aloud so that the children understand why you are choosing to write about some parts of the diagram and not about other parts.

It is important that I say how many bricks there are and what kind of slope it is – I think this is a gentle slope. So I am going to write **This is a gentle slope because the ramp is on top of two bricks.** I haven't just said that it is a gentle slope, I've also explained why it is a gentle slope.

**TEACHER SCRIBING**

● Ask the children to help you to finish your explanation for this first picture.

How did the car run down this slope? … Did it go fast or quite slowly? … Let's write that … Now we need to say why the car only went slowly down this ramp …. Let's read what we've written. **The car went slowly down the ramp. It wasn't a steep slope.** Can anyone tell me a conjunction I could use to join the sentences? … **The car went slowly down the ramp, but it wasn't a steep slope.** Do you think **but** is a good conjunction to use here? … Does **but** begin an explanation of why the car went slowly down the slope? No, **but** suggests that we are surprised that the car went slowly down the slope. Let's try using **as** or **because** – those are conjunctions which introduce an explanation. They are called 'cause and effect' conjunctions.

● Refer back to some of the examples from shared reading to help the children to recognise that cause and effect conjunctions like **because** can be used to explain why something happens.

## Independent work

● The children can begin work on a booklet of explanations. They could begin to plan the contents and write the contents page.
● With a teaching assistant, the children can continue some investigations. The teaching assistant should encourage explanatory talk from the children.
● The children can draw and label their own diagrams to show the experiment of the cars and the ramps.

## Plenary

● The children who have been working with the teaching assistant can report back on what they find, giving explanations for what they observed.
● Let other children give explanations for things they know and understand. They could be related to the experiments you have been doing or not. The important issue is whether they include an explanation of why something happens, not simply a report that it does happen.

## Session 2
### Talk for writing

● Reconstruct the text you composed together at the last session and write it so the children can see it, eg:

This is a gentle slope because the ramp is only on top of two bricks.
The car went slowly down the ramp because it was only a gentle slope.

Can anyone tell me which conjunction we have used in these sentences? Can you underline them? Why have we used because rather than and or but? … Because is a conjunction which tells you **why** something happened.

● Use strips of card like the following to play a game of Construct.

| Blue strips | Green strips |
|---|---|
| The car goes faster down the higher ramp because | it's going down a steeper slope. |
| The car goes faster down the higher ramp so | it reaches the bottom of the ramp more quickly. |
| The car goes faster down the higher ramp and | its wheels go round faster too. |
| The car goes faster down the higher ramp but | it would go even faster down an even higher one. |

● Give a strip of card to each of eight children. Ask them to find the person with the strip that makes the best sentence with their strip. Once all the children have found a partner, ask the rest of the children to decide whether the children have made the best sentences. Can any of the children spot the word on the blue strips which decides which of the green strips is most appropriate? Ask them: 'Which of the conjunctions on the blue strips tells us why something happened?'

## Shared writing
SUPPORTED COMPOSITION

● The children have dry-wipe boards (one between two). Show them again the text you worked out together in the last session and read it together. Refer to the diagram of the lower ramp which now has the two sentences displayed under it which you compiled in Session 1. Remind the children that you wrote two sentences – one to explain why the slope is gentle, and the other to explain why the car travelled slowly. Now refer them to the diagram of the higher ramp and ask the children to work in their pairs to think of the writing that could go under the diagram. Tell them not to write anything yet, but ask them to work out *what* they are going to write.

● Ask them to tell their partner what they have planned to write.

● Before any of the children write, ask some of them to tell the others what they have planned that they are going to write. Help those that need it to recast their sentences into short explanations. Keep repeating the word because and congratulating children who have used it.

UNIT **13**

- Let the children write their brief explanations about why the car went fast down the higher ramp. Remind them to keep on rereading their writing as they work, checking that their writing makes sense and that their spelling and punctuation is good.
- Let some of the children read their explanations out to the class.

## Independent work

Ask all the children to draw two diagrams, one showing the car coming down a gentle slope and the other showing it coming down a steep slope. The children should label their diagrams and write simple explanations under them. Remind them that when they write an explanation:

- They should describe what they saw using language like **The ramp is higher**, and try not to use the words **I** or **we**. This is like writing a report.
- They must try to explain *why* the car went faster. When they write an explanation, they will probably need to use the connective **because**

### GUIDED WRITING

The teacher could work with one group to either support or extend their writing. Less confident writers could use the card strips from the Construct game to help them to structure their sentences. Ask more confident writers to extend their writing to suggest other ways in which cars could be made to go faster and to explain why they would work.

## Plenary

- Ask the children what they think is important about an explanation. Be positive about responses which refer to why something happens.
- Can the children remember a useful connective which introduces *why* information?
- Ask some of the children to read their explanations aloud, while others listen to see if they have explained why the car travels fast down the higher ramp.
- Talk about the use of the diagrams. Are they helpful, or would the explanation have worked just as well without them?

*You may wish to repeat parts of this unit in the context of further writing of explanatory text.*

## Session 3
### Talk for writing

- Show the children some glossaries in the back of information books. Ask the following questions:

> - What is a glossary for? … How is it different from a normal dictionary?
> - How do authors decide which words to put in the glossary?
> - How do authors decide which order to put the words in? … Why is this a more sensible way to order the words than just writing them in the order that they come in the book?

- Look at the different length of definitions in the different glossaries and compare the kind of information that is given.

● Talk about definitions.

> Why wouldn't it be any use to say a ramp is a ramp? … Is this a good definition for a ramp … A ramp is a piece of wood? Can anybody think of a better one?

## Shared writing

Tell the children that you are going to begin to work on a glossary for the back of their science booklet. In this example, the glossary will cover the list of technical terms compiled from the science experiments.

TEACHER DEMONSTRATION

> I'm going to begin to write a definition for the word ramp. What do I think people need to know about a ramp? I think they need to know what it looks like, what it is made of, what it is used for and how it is used. I think I'll make a list so that I can use it to help me remember all the things I need to say … I think I'll begin by writing A ramp is a long, flat piece of wood. It must be wide enough for a toy car to go down.

Ask the children which features of the definition they think you have covered. Put a tick beside them on your list. Ask them what they need to write about next and to find out what it is used for.

## Session 4
## Shared writing
TEACHER SCRIBING

● Ask the children to help you with the next bit of your definition. (If necessary, focus the children's thoughts on the kind of ramps you used in class, not on those for coming off motorways or down multi-storey car parks!) Let them offer ideas to begin with, then help them to formulate their ideas into sentences, eg It is used in experiments to see what makes cars travel faster; it is used so that wheelchairs/pushchairs can get up and down the front steps ….
● If you have begun by describing 'a ramp', make sure that the children don't change it to 'ramps'.
● As you scribe their ideas, keep on rereading and evaluating what you are writing. Some of the children may be able to help you with high frequency words, or with adding punctuation.
● When you have finished writing, reread the definition so far to check that it makes sense.
● Tick off 'what it is used for' on your list.

SUPPORTED COMPOSITION

- Ask the children to discuss the final point for the definition – 'How it is used' – with their partner. Tell them that they should first agree on the kind of information that needs to be given, and then try to say it in sentences. Monitor the children's work, helping any who are experiencing problems.

> What's the question you are thinking about? …
> Do you remember when we did the experiment with the cars?
> What did we do with the ramp? How did we use it? … Good. Can
> you say that in a sentence? … Perhaps your sentence could begin
> **The ramp is ….** How would you finish it?

- Let some of the children share their ideas with the class before anyone begins to write.
- As the children begin to write their ideas, remind them to keep rereading their writing, improving it where necessary.

## Independent work

- The children should compile a list of words they think they need to gloss from the experiments they have written in their booklet. If they have only done the car experiment, they should try to write definitions for **slope** and **car** as well as **ramp**.
- The children should list their words in alphabetical order on their dry-wipe boards before they begin to write any definitions.
- Let the children write two or three words in their glossary.

## Plenary

- Remind the children about the need to write the word **Glossary** as a heading for the page.
- Let the children read aloud their glossary definitions and see if the other children can say what the word is each time.
- Check for coverage of list of things to be covered.

## What next?

- The children could continue to make their booklet to explain further science experiments.
- As the children write in other curriculum areas, help them to recognise which text type they are using and why. Explanations are most likely to be used in science and maths.
- Encourage children to use explanations accompanied by diagrams/numbered sentences in the 'solving problems' topic of the numeracy strategy (see *Framework for teaching mathematics*, Section 5 pages 66–70).

# UNIT 14
# Y2 Term 3: Nonsense Verse

**Target:** Use poetry structures and language when writing
**Pupil target:** I can write my own poems, based on poems I enjoy reading. I can choose the words I use carefully.
**Outcome:** A verse of a humorous poem, based on a shared poem
**Range:** Texts with language play, eg riddles/tongue twisters, humorous verse and stories

## OBJECTIVES

| | |
|---|---|
| **T8** | to discuss meanings of words and phrases that create humour and sound effects in poetry …; |
| **T9** | to apply phonological, graphic knowledge and sight vocabulary to spell words accurately; |
| **T11** | to use humorous verse as a structure for children to write their own by adaptation, mimicry or substitution; |
| **S2** | the need for grammatical agreement …; |
| **S3** | to use standard forms of verbs in speaking and writing …; |
| **W10** | to use synonyms and other alternative words/phrases that express same or similar meanings …; |

**QCA Music Scheme of work**
The context for and content of children's writing could be enhanced by connecting this unit to the QCA Music Scheme of Work, Unit 2: Sounds interesting, which involves children in creating sounds in response to descriptive words.

## Purpose and context

Writing will arise from reading a variety of different kinds of humorous writing, including poetry.

- Help the children to develop an understanding of why they like particular poems. Ask them if they like the subject of the poem – or the language. Ask whether there are any words or lines they think are particularly good? Ask someone to read them aloud so the rest of the class can enjoy them too.
- During discussion, use some of the technical language the children will need to talk about what they are reading. The NLS Technical Vocabulary List for Year 2 includes the words: **nonsense poem**, **riddle**, **scan**, **syllable**, **tongue-twister**, **verse**, and the words **rhyme** and **sound** have been used since Reception. Able children may also enjoy learning about **alliteration** which is formally introduced in Year 3. The more familiar the children are with these terms, the more easily they will discuss them, developing their understanding of the use and effect of patterning in poetry. These technical terms shouldn't hold any fear for the children if they are always used in context, and you gloss their meaning in a natural way, eg 'How many syllables are there in "apple"? How many times would you tap your finger to tap out its rhythm? Two.'
- Many poems are most effective when they are read aloud. Humour which relies on punning and ambiguity is only really effective when read aloud. Encourage the children to share poems they enjoy with their friends by reading them aloud as well as by putting them into a class anthology.

## Session 1
### Talk for writing

- Read together the poem that you plan to use for your model. These ideas are all based on the poem 'The Apple and the Worm' by Robert Heidbreder (which can be found in *Nonsense! Poems* chosen by Richard Brown and Kate Ruttle, published by CUP as part of Cambridge Reading), but the ideas can be adapted for other poems.

- Ask the children what makes this poem funny? Start by talking about the content of the poem, about the idea of eating an apple with a worm inside it. Do the children understand the last line?

- Talk about the patterning and the language in the poem. Ask the children which words rhyme, or end with the same sounds, and which words begin with the same sounds, or alliterate.

- Write the word **worm** and ask the children which words they can find that describe how the worm moves or feels? Show the children how to make a 'word-web' using words to describe worms, then talk about how the poet has used the words in the poem. Ask which lines in the poem tell us what the worm feels like as it goes down into the person's tummy.

- Ask the children to think of another minibeast they might find in an apple, eg an ant or a beetle. Begin to construct a word-web to describe how the minibeast might move, look or feel.

- Tell them that they are going to try to write a second verse for this poem. In the second verse, the person can be eating a different food. Ask someone to suggest one and also to suggest what might be in it.

### Shared writing
TEACHER DEMONSTRATION

The children will need to be able to see the original poem throughout the shared writing session.

- Remind them that they decided that the verse was going to be about someone eating a bun with a beetle in it. So they will need to alter it to show what they are eating.

- Write the first four lines, talking aloud to explain which words you are replacing and why.

> I am going to use the layout and punctuation of the original poem. Remember that in poetry new lines often begin with capital letters, even though they're not the beginnings of sentences.

TEACHER SCRIBING

> The next four lines in the original poem are all about how the worm moved inside, so we need to look at movement words on our word-web. At the moment we're not going to worry about making the poem rhyme. Which words are we going to have to replace? … The last word on each line. … Look at the movement words on our word-web and think about which ones you would like to use. (eg scurry, hurry, scramble, scrabble, stumble) Who can suggest what the next line should be?

- Write the next four lines, replacing the last word on each line with a new word the children suggest from your word-web.

SUPPORTED COMPOSITION

- The children can use their dry-wipe boards and work in pairs to suggest how the next two lines – which describe how the creature feels – could go. They will need to find three good words from your word-web, or they could add other words if they can think of them, eg **hard**, **scaly**, **shiny**, **crunchy**. When they have written the lines, ask them:
    - to read them aloud and talk about them;
    - to decide whether the words sound right and are in the best order;
    - to try them in a different order and see;
    - if they can use alliteration, words that begin with the same sound;
    - if any of their words rhyme with **tummy**, and if so where they would put them in their poem to make a rhyme;
    - if they could replace any of their words with any better words.
- Share the children's ideas and agree on the best words.

> Who would like to read out their lines?
> I think the way you've done … is very good. Perhaps you could think of a different word instead of …? Can anyone suggest a better word? … Would anyone else like to read their lines? … We've heard several good ideas. A lot of you have used the line …, so let's add that to our class poem. Write the lines on your class poem and then add the ending from the original poem.

- As a class, read your poem aloud, trying out your new verse. Can the children suggest any better words anywhere?

## Independent work

- Work with a teaching assistant and a collection of percussion instruments to add sound effects, either to the original verse or to your new verse.
- A group can think of a different minibeast, eg a slug, a ladybird, a butterfly and compile a word-web to show its movements and how it feels. Show the children how to use thesauruses to gain access to a wider vocabulary. Talk about whether the words they find are true synonyms or not.
- A group can edit the class verse, trying to see if it can be made to rhyme by swapping some of the words around or by adding new words.
- Let children use the original poem. Give them different coloured pencils and ask them to underline different sets of words in different colours, eg movement words in blue, feeling words in red, words that begin with **s** in yellow, rhyming words in green, etc. This activity should help children to become more aware of language and organisation in the poem.
- Let children look through poetry anthologies, finding and sharing those they find humorous.

## Plenary

- If any of the editors think they have improved the class poem, encourage them to read out their ideas for the rest of the children to evaluate.
- Children who have been exploring the poem with sound effects can do a performance. When they have performed once, let them explain why they chose the sounds they did to accompany each of the words and then perform the poem again to demonstrate the effectiveness of their choices.
- Discuss, briefly, how the sound effects and patterning in the words in the poem contribute to the reader's enjoyment of it.

## Session 2
### Talk for writing

- Again, read together the poem that you plan to use for your model. These ideas are all based on the poem 'On the Ning Nang Nong' by Spike Milligan (which can also be found in *Nonsense! Poems* chosen by Richard Brown and Kate Ruttle, published by CUP as part of Cambridge Reading), but the ideas can be adapted for other poems.

- Prepare a copy of the poem for the children to edit as part of a Replace activity. Let the children see the poem clearly and ask them if there is one cow, or more than one cow on the Ning, Nang, Nong? How do they know? How would the line 'Where the Cows go Bong!' have to change if there was only one cow? Once the children have changed **Cows** to **Cow** ask them to read the line again. What else needs to change to make the line grammatically correct?

> The verb, the word that tells us what is happening in a sentence, tells us both when the action in a sentence happens, or happened (the tense) and how many people or things are involved. If there is more than one person, or thing, we need to use a plural form of the verb, eg **The Cows go Bong**. If there is only one person or thing, we need to use a different form of the verb, eg **The Cow goes Bong**.

- Ask the children to look at the rest of the poem and together edit it to change all the plural forms into singular ones. Encourage the children to look for the plural nouns first (these should be familiar from term 2's word level work) and then ask them to repeat the sentence, listening and thinking about how to change the verb form.

- Reread 'On the Ning Nang Nong' and tell the children that you're going to write your own version. It's a good poem to use as a scaffold, because rhythm and rhyme are easy, since the poem doesn't have to make sense! Agree a title for your poem, eg **The Bing Bang Bong**.

- Before you begin your own version, use different coloured pencils to work out the rhyming structure of the original poem. Draw circles round pairs of rhyming words, using a coloured line to link the rhymes at the ends of the third, sixth and ninth lines.

### Shared writing
TEACHER DEMONSTRATION

The children will need to be able to see the original poem to use it as a scaffold throughout the session.

- Write the first line of your poem, using the title agreed earlier.

> What kind of creature might live here? Perhaps **a hen that goes wrong**? Or **hens that go pong**? I need to end this line with an **-ong** word to rhyme with **Bong** in the first line. And I need to decide whether I'm going to have one or more hen. I'm going to read aloud the first two lines and decide which sounds better, **hens that go pong** or **a hen going wrong**. The third line needs a different rhyme at the end, because it's got to rhyme with the sixth and ninth lines. I think I might keep **Boo** at the end of this line, to keep it easy. But what will I have that says 'Boo'? A hippo or hippos?

● Once you have finished writing three lines, reread your work, exploring other possibilities as you do so. Keep the rhythm going so that the children can hear if lines don't scan.

TEACHER SCRIBING
● Let the children help you to work on the next three lines. Encourage them to try out different ideas and versions and remind them that even after you've written an idea down, it's not too late to change it for a better one.
● This structure can be very useful for encouraging reluctant spellers to try spelling new words on your version. They can use a variety of strategies, particularly rhyme, to help them work out spellings.

## Independent work

The children have dry-wipe boards (one between two). They can write the final three lines in their pairs. They need to talk about their ideas, trying them out orally before they commit them to writing. As the children write, enccurage them to keep rereading their lines aloud to see if they are good.

## What next?

The children can work in pairs to write their own version of 'On the Ning Nang Nong'. They can decide for themselves how much of the original to retain. Before they begin, remind them to:

● think about the rhythm and rhyme of the original poem and try to copy it;
● think about whether they want to have one or more than one of each of their creatures and consider what that means for the verb each time;
● use the rhymes to support their spelling;
● consider each line carefully before they write it down, then to reread their poems constantly to decide if they can be improved.

# UNIT 15
# Y2 Term 3: Non-chronological Report

**Target:** Begin to show characteristics of non-chronological report, incorporating appropriate language to sequence and categorise ideas

**Pupil target:** I can ask questions to find out information and I can write a report text which includes the information.

**Outcome:** A short report text about babies and children

**Range:** Information books including non-chronological reports

## OBJECTIVES

| | |
|---|---|
| **T14** | to pose questions and record these in writing, prior to reading non-fiction to find answers; |
| **T19** | to make simple notes from non-fiction texts, e.g. key words and phrases, headings, page references …; |
| **T20** | to write non-fiction texts, using text read as models for own writing …; |
| **T21** | to write non-chronological reports based on structure of known texts, … using appropriate language …; |
| **S4** | to use commas in lists; |
| **S5** | to write in clear sentences, using capital letters and full stops accurately; |
| **S6** | to turn statements into questions, learning a range of wh- words; |

**QCA Science Scheme of work**
Content of and context for writing can be provided by linking this unit to Unit 2A: Health and growth, which requires children to raise questions in order to make comparisons and to describe differences observed, eg between babies and toddlers.

## Purpose and context

Before the writing sessions, the children should have:

- read a variety of non-chronological report texts and discussed their features (a summary of the main features of report text can be found in Section 2 in Part 3 of this book);
- identified some of the technical terms needed to discuss report texts including: **diagram**, **heading**, **key phrase**, **key word**, **layout**, **non-chronological**, **sub-heading** (these terms are in the NLS Technical Vocabulary Lists for Years 1 and 2);
- developed a familiarity with structural guiders in information books, eg index, contents, headings, etc.;
- found books about toddlers and babies and looked through them;
- discussed personal experience of babies/toddlers and collected photographs, artefacts and information in a class exhibition.

## Session 1
### Talk for writing

- To begin to help the children to think about question forms, use strips of card with the following words and punctuation as the basis for a Reorder activity.

| Where | does | The baby | eat |
|-------|------|----------|-----|
| What | can | The toddler | drink |
| When | | | need to be carried |
| Which | . | | need to be fed |
| Who | ? | | want to cuddle |
| Why | s | | cry |
| How | | | play |

- Cut out all the card strips. You can either use a washing line, or ask the children to hold the strips.
- Use the cards to make a statement, eg **The baby** + **eat** + **s** + . Can any of the children use other cards to change your sentence into a question? Eg **Why** + **does** + **The baby** + **eat** + **?**
- Discuss how the statement has been changed to make it into a question, raising issues like:
  - Which new words have we added to the statement to make it into a question?
  - Which words have we changed?
  - How has the punctuation changed?
  - Are there any other things we should change to make this a good question? (Remove the extra capital letter.)
  - Can anyone think of different questions we could make from the same statement?
  - Which words will we have to change to ask the new questions?
  - How is the meaning of the question different now that we have changed the **wh-**, question word?
- Tell the children that you are going to collect information about babies and toddlers and then you are going to work together to write a report about how you look after them.

## Session 2
### Shared writing
You will need a marker pen and Post-it notes or paper and Blu-tak for this session.

TEACHER DEMONSTRATION
Refer the children to the list of question starter words used earlier. Model writing a simple question about caring for babies and toddlers on a Post-it note. As you write your question, think aloud to make your thoughts explicit.

I wonder why babies cry at night. How can I make that into a question? What is it I really want to know? Do I want to know why babies cry, or when babies cry? Am I more interested in the reasons for babies crying (**why** they cry) or the time that they cry (**when** they cry)? I think I want to know **why** they cry. So I'll begin my question with a capital letter for Why and write Why do babies cry and of course I need to end with a question mark.

**TEACHER SCRIBING**

- Ask the children what they would like to find out about babies and toddlers.

> Before we begin to write our report, we will need to decide what kind of information to include in the report. So, to begin with, I want you to think of questions we could find answers to. For instance, I might want to know about babies being carried, but toddlers walking. I can use the sentences and questions we used before to help me to ask a question. I think my question is a when question, because I think what I want to know is when do babies start to walk?

- Ask the children to turn to their neighbour and to quietly agree on some questions to ask. They could use some of the sentence structures from the Reorder activity as a guide.
- When the children have discussed their ideas, ask some of them to tell you their questions. As you scribe on Post-it notes, ask the children to remind you about punctuation.

**SUPPORTED COMPOSITION**

- The children should work in pairs, on their dry-wipe boards, to write some of the questions they want to find answers to. Explain that one of them should write the question, then the other one in the pair should read it and make sure that it is correct and that the punctuation is right. When they have agreed on that question, swap over so that the other person writes.
- Ask each pair to decide which is their most interesting question. Let them read it aloud to the others. Through your response, help the children to refine their questions.

> That's an interesting question, but I'm not sure what kind of information you are expecting to find. Is your question really about why babies learn to walk? Or are you interested in how or when babies learn to walk? Remember, why questions expect a reason to be given. A how question would find out what stages babies go though as they learn to walk. A when question would find out how old babies are when they begin to walk. What do you want to find out? ... Can anybody suggest a question to find out this information?

## Independent work

- Let the children stick their Post-it note questions to the front of a book which they think will have the information they need. Ask them to read the book and to write the page number which has the answer on it on the Post-it note.
- A teaching assistant can work with a group of children looking at photographs of the members of the class as toddlers and babies or at commercial pictures/posters. The teaching assistant should encourage discussion about the different needs of the babies and toddlers as shown in the pictures and how those needs are met by their carers.
- The children can begin to make lists of things that babies need or things that toddlers need. Remind them to use commas to separate items in a list.
- The children could draw and label some of the things that babies need and beside them draw and label the equivalent thing that a toddler needs.

## Plenary

- Children who have been finding information in books could read aloud both their question and the answer they found.
- Other children can choose a question to which they already know the answer, read the question aloud, then supply their answer. Encourage shy children or less confident readers who have younger siblings to answer the questions on the grounds that they have expertise that some other children don't have.

## Session 3

### Talk for writing

- Prepare a short report text about babies and toddlers. Write each sentence on a strip of paper, but don't organise the information properly. For example:

| |
|---|
| Babies need milk to drink. |
| Toddlers wear pants, but they sometimes wet themselves. |
| Toddlers drink their milk from training beakers. |
| Babies need to be carried because they can't walk themselves. |
| Babies wear nappies. |
| Babies can't eat solid food because they don't have any teeth. |
| Toddlers usually use potties when they want to go to the toilet. |
| Toddlers can walk, but they fall over quite a lot. |
| Toddlers can eat the same food as adults, but it needs to be cut up into small pieces. |
| Babies drink their milk from bottles. |

- Read the sentences aloud with the children.

> What kind of information about babies and toddlers can we find from this report text? What babies and toddlers eat and drink, how they go to the toilet and how they get around. We can use different coloured highlighter pens to find the bits of information which should go together. Let's decide which sentences should be highlighted in the same colour. ... Now that we have highlighted the information, can anybody suggest a better way of organising it? Would it make more sense if all the information about the same topic was put together? ... Does it matter which topic we choose first?

- Using colours to underline or highlight like this is a very useful note-making strategy.

## Session 4
### Shared writing
TEACHER DEMONSTRATION

> Now that we have reorganised this text, we need to add sub-headings to each section so that people can find information quickly and easily. Questions make very good sub-headings. I'm going to read all the information in this section and then I'll think about a sub-heading for it. All of this section tells me about what babies and toddlers like to eat and drink. How can I make that into a question? I'll use a **wh-** question word to start. I think **what** is the best one. So my sub-heading is **What do babies and toddlers like to eat?** I need to remember to begin my question with a capital letter and finish it with a question mark.

TEACHER SCRIBING

- Ask the children if they can think of questions which can act as sub-headings for each of the other sections in the report text. Remind them that before they put their hands up they should:
  - read all the information in the section;
  - decide what it's about;
  - think about which wh- question word you might want to use at the beginning of your question. 'Don't forget about our list which reminds you which words we can use for questions.'
- Give the children time to think before letting them give answers. Ask them to tell you what the information in the section is about before they try to formulate the question.

> Good. This section is about babies and toddlers eating and drinking. Which **wh-** question word did you think was best? … Does anyone else have a different idea? … Look carefully at the information. Are we told **what** babies and toddlers eat and drink or **why** they need to eat and drink? Which question word would be best? How would you finish the question?

SUPPORTED COMPOSITION

- The children have dry-wipe boards (one between two). Ask the children to talk with their partner about some aspect of the lives of babies and children and agree three or four things they know about it, eg toys, where they sleep, how they go out for walks, what they wear, how much they cry, etc. Remind them that if they are stuck, they should think about the questions they made in the last session or use ideas from the beginning of this session.
- When they have agreed what their subject is, they should write their ideas in sentences (remembering to punctuate their sentences properly) and think of a question as a sub-heading. As the children are writing, move around the class, encouraging children to reread what they have written. Ask them to check the following: 'Does each sentence make sense? Is all the information you have given about the same topic, or do you think you are thinking about two different topics? What is the question you are trying to answer?'

● Let the children read some of their report texts aloud. Encourage peer response, using the model of saying something that you like and then some way in which the text could be improved.

## Independent work

● Ask the children to use the writing they have just done as the first section of a report text about babies and toddlers. They should put the heading **Babies and toddlers** at the top of their page, then write out the section they have just worked on. Then, they should try to add at least one other section, preferably two or three more. Each section should consist of:
  – three of four sentences which give linked information;
  – a question for a sub-title.
● Remind them to think about what they want to say before they write it down, and to reread each section carefully to check that it makes sense and that the sentences are properly punctuated.

### GUIDED WRITING

The teacher could work with one group to either support or extend their writing. Less able children can base their report on the one you used at the beginning of the session. Encourage them to use pronouns and connectives to link the ideas more coherently. Help more able children to look at language use and begin to use a more formal style of writing.

## Plenary

Ask children to check their own writing while you read out a checklist of desirable features.

> Check that you have:
>
> ● written and underlined your heading Babies and toddlers;
> ● written questions as sub-headings for each section, and used a capital letter to begin each question and a question mark at the end;
> ● used sentences in your writing. Each sentence must begin with a capital letter and end with a full stop;
> ● written sentences that make sense. If you like, you can give your work to a friend and ask them to read your sentences through for you.

Give the children a few minutes to check that they have done all these things.

## What next?

● The children could develop their report text into a little illustrated booklet about babies and toddlers. They could add new information about children and adults or about other animals and their babies.
● Start a 'question wall' in your classroom where children can write up any question that occurs to them. You, or any of the children, can post answers to the questions. This encourages children to pose focused questions as well as to use information books or the Internet to find answers.
● Encourage the children to write specific questions before they begin to browse for information in information books, otherwise they are likely to get sidetracked.

# Sentence level units

In Year 2, children harness their ideas into discrete simple, compound and complex sentences. They have an increasing need to understand basic principles of punctuation including those relating to written dialogue. They need the ability to impose a coherence on text as they write recounts, stories, reports, etc. Focusing on these aspects of sentence level work before applying this knowledge to writing will be beneficial. This approach is taken in *Grammar for writing* (DfEE 2000) at Key Stage 2. All the Year 2 sentence level objectives which relate to writing are addressed in the next nine units (Units A–I).

## How to use the teaching units

**NLS objective**

### Principles and explanation

This section defines principles, rules or conventions, as appropriate. Full definitions for all grammatical terminology used in the National Literacy Strategy *Framework for teaching* can be found in the revised version of the Glossary on the disk accompanying this book and also on the DfEE Standards site: http://www. standards.dfee.gov.uk/literacy/glossary/. There may also be teaching points about aspects of the objective children tend to find difficult and an explanation of the importance of the objective to writing.

### Sentence level activities

This section contains a number of activities which will further children's understanding of the content of the objective. Some of these activities are described in full. Others are only given a name (eg Function, Collect and classify) because the generic instructions for these are given on pages 128–30 of this book.

---

*Unit A Y2 Term 1*

## UNIT A
## Y2 Term 1 S2, T4 and T11

**OBJECTIVES**

| | |
|---|---|
| **S2** | to find examples, in fiction and non-fiction, of words and phrases that link sentences; |
| **T4** | to understand time and sequential relationships in stories, i.e. what happened when; |
| **T11** | to use language of time to structure a sequence of events, e.g. 'when I finished ...', 'suddenly ...', 'after that ...'. |

### Principles and explanation

- Some words and phrases at the start of sentences help to link or connect sentences together so that sentences follow on from each other in a time sequence, eg later on, suddenly, after that, finally, first, next, later, meanwhile, then, after a while, when I finished.
- Children often use and then to link ideas, which can be boring. To avoid using and then start a new sentence, join the sentences or start a new sentence with a connecting word or phrase, eg:
  They saw the dogs and then they looked at the cows could become:
  They saw the dogs. Then they looked at the cows.
  After they saw the dogs, they looked at the cows.
  They saw the dogs. After that, they looked at the cows.
- Constant rereading and retelling of stories helps embed writing structures rather than speech patterns.

### Sentence level activities
**Compare (page 128)**

**Version 1**
Jodie went outside and it was sunny and then she sat on the doorstep and waited and then she saw Mrs Bucket going up the street to the shop and then she saw Sandy ride past on his bike and he wobbled so much that Jodie had to laugh and then she saw the postman and then it was Milko visiting each house with one or two pints and then she saw Mrs Bucket come out of the shop and then Jodie saw that Mrs Bucket was struggling with two large shopping bags and then she ran to help.

**Version 2**
Jodie went outside. It was sunny, so she sat on the doorstep and waited. First she saw Mrs Bucket going up the street to the shop. A little later on she saw Sandy ride past on his bike. He wobbled so much that Jodie had to laugh. Next she saw the postman. Later on it was Milko visiting each house with one or two pints. Finally, she saw Mrs Bucket come out of the shop. When Jodie saw that Mrs Bucket was struggling with two large shopping bags she ran to help.

**Collect and classify (page 128)**
List the connectives used in version 2 of the Compare activity above. Continue to collect from fiction and non-fiction texts over the next weeks. Make two lists – fiction and non-fiction and indicate the type of non-fiction text, eg instructions.

**Oral**
Use linking words and phrases when carrying out everyday tasks, eg First, we'll do the register. After that we'll settle down to some work.

132

---

Generic activity and page number for instructions. Many of the activities are repeated so general instructions are included on pages 128–30 of this book. Specific material and variations for carrying out the activity are included here.

# Planning

The activities are intended to be carried out in the 15-minute sentence level time in the Literacy Hour. You may well find that you can do two of the sentence level activities in the 15 minutes. Alternatively, you may do one and start another, leaving the children to complete it in the independent session, and then return to it in the plenary. None of these activities is complete without the children articulating what they have learned both about the principles of the language feature or the sentence structure they have been considering, and the implications of this knowledge for their own writing. You may wish to put the sentence level activity straight into practice in shared writing during the following 15 minutes.

A choice of sentence level activities is included in each teaching unit. You may need to carry out just one activity with your classes, whereas other classes may need to do all the activities and more to give the children adequate practice. But the aim is to move into applying the sentence level skills and knowledge in writing, not to get stuck on activities.

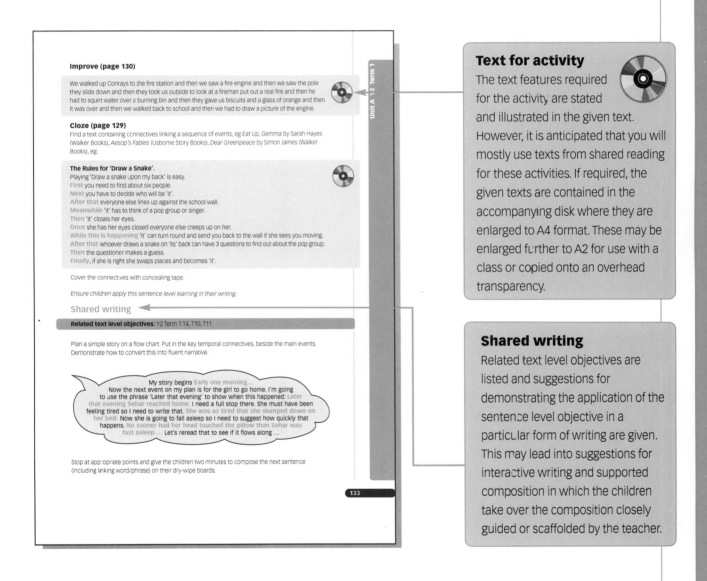

### Text for activity

The text features required for the activity are stated and illustrated in the given text. However, it is anticipated that you will mostly use texts from shared reading for these activities. If required, the given texts are contained in the accompanying disk where they are enlarged to A4 format. These may be enlarged further to A2 for use with a class or copied onto an overhead transparency.

### Shared writing

Related text level objectives are listed and suggestions for demonstrating the application of the sentence level objective in a particular form of writing are given. This may lead into suggestions for interactive writing and supported composition in which the children take over the composition closely guided or scaffolded by the teacher.

# Teaching sentence level activities

- Each teaching unit provides a number of different possible activities to help deepen children's understanding of the sentence level objectives. These activities provide the basis for investigation and discussion about how language is constructed and used effectively in written forms.

- These activities involve the whole class and require the active, brisk participation of the children.

- Children will be motivated by the investigative nature of these activities, but they will need help in articulating their deductions from the investigations.

- There is a choice of activity in each unit. The number of activities you choose to do will depend on the previous experience of the children. However, it is important not to spend longer than necessary on these activities, as it is the application of the principles in shared and independent writing which is the ultimate object of sentence level work.

- Some activities are used repeatedly in different teaching units. The generic instructions for these activities are on pages 128–30. Additional instructions and the text, sentences or words for the activity are included in the teaching unit.

- Many of the activities use texts. An example of a suitable text is often included in the teaching unit, but it is expected that you will wish to use a page of text from a book you are using in shared reading, or one the children have already read. Usually the text needs to be marked either before or during the activity. It is possible to mark text by covering the page in the book with a sheet of acetate and using a water soluble pen or using removable highlighting tape.

- Many of the activities suggest that children use hand-held dry-wipe boards. The purpose is to involve all members of the class. Usually it is adequate to have one between two children. They take turns in writing. They both discuss what to write. While one writes, the other checks for accuracy. At a cue from the teacher, the children hold up their dry-wipe boards. The teacher scans them quickly, assessing the level of response and deciding on the next teaching move. Sometimes it will be appropriate to take a correct answer and move on. At other times, the teacher may wish to choose an answer which indicates a misconception which is shared by a number of the children and take the opportunity to do some corrective teaching.

- During the activities, help the children to see the relationship between different examples of the focused grammatical feature, eg nouns, and draw out from them the underlying principles governing its use and effect in writing. Avoid telling the children the principles at the outset, but ensure they have all grasped them by the end of the activity.

- At the end of the activity, ask the children to summarise what they have learned about the particular focus element they have been investigating. Sometimes, this can be done first in pairs or threes, using dry-wipe boards to ensure maximum involvement, before entering a class discussion.

- The principles, generalisations or explanation which they have, with your guidance, extracted from the activity should be written on a poster as a reminder for when they use this element in their own writing.

- You should also plan to include references to this element in future teaching.

- Expect children to use what they have learned from these activities in their writing, not only in any immediate follow-up independent writing, but in all their subsequent writing where appropriate.

# Teaching writing

**Sample sequence: Year 2, Term 2, S7:** to investigate and recognise a range of other ways of presenting texts, eg speech bubbles, enlarged, bold or italicised print, captions, headings and sub-headings.

**1 Sentence level teaching focus** – putting the spotlight on the objective and introducing it to the class.

**2 Sentence level activities** – interactive whole class activities for maximum involvement using 'show me' and 'get up and go' techniques. Activities include collecting and categorising, transforming, substituting, deleting and predicting, constructing rules and explanations.

**3 Define principles** –
working with the children to
define their understanding of the
objective. Ask children to
articulate what they have
learned. They should be able to:

- provide a definition (eg of an
  adjective), and also
- say something about how it
  is used.

**4 Teacher
demonstration
and scribing** –
demonstrating
writing in front of
the children, talking
them through the
process, and
showing how to
employ the
objective within the
course of a fluent
piece of writing.
Children may be
involved in helping
you compose – but
always keep up the
explanatory
commentary and
maintain the focus
upon the objective
in use.

*As well as focusing on the day's objective, continually demonstrate how to:*

- *rehearse sentences in speech before committing them to paper;*
- *frequently reread the text during writing to maintain fluency and spot any errors;*
- *reread at the end to check for coherence and accuracy.*

**5 Support composition** – helping children focus on the objective as they try their hand at a short piece of writing. This may involve sentence-makers for young children, working on a dry-wipe board or collaborative writing.

**6 Independent writing** – the children write a text, focusing upon the objective.

**7 Review**

– marking and response are carefully focused by the objective. You can now use examples from children's work to make further teaching points. It may be worth asking several children to work straight onto an overhead transparency, so that in the plenary several examples can be reviewed to see what has worked and where improvements might be made.

## Instructions for generic sentence level activities

Certain activities can be used for different purposes. To save space the instructions for these are given below.

### Function

PURPOSE

To give children the opportunity to investigate the function of a word class, sentence structure or punctuation mark.

RESOURCES

Page of enlarged text with all the words (approximately 10) of the particular focus, eg adjectives, marked or highlighted and one word near the end which is highlighted but not in the word class.

INSTRUCTIONS
- Tell the children the objective of the lesson.
- Read through the text and then read again the first sentence which contains a highlighted word.
- Discuss the function of the highlighted word in the text, eg **the wise man** – **wise** is telling us more about **the man**.
- Ask the children to discuss in pairs the function of the next highlighted word; take responses.
- Relate the function of this word to the function of the first word to see the commonality.
- Do the same with the next few words until you are sure that most children have understood.
- Tell them the name of the word class if no one has suggested it already.
- Ask the children to carry on to the end to find the highlighted word which is not in the same class.

FOLLOW-UP

The children can look out for words in this category in their reading.

### Collect and classify

PURPOSES
- To give children practice in identifying elements such as word class, sentence structure or punctuation mark.
- To give children the opportunity to investigate their subtypes or different functions.

RESOURCES

Depending on the objective, either a page of enlarged text containing a number of examples of the feature to be taught, or a collection of examples from a number of texts.

INSTRUCTIONS
- Tell the children the objective of the lesson and highlight the first two examples of the focus for the activity.
- Ask the children to name the focus element, eg commas.
- The specific objective: suggest at least two categories for classifying the examples of the element into, eg commas in lists, commas to signal a grammatical boundary.

### Compare

PURPOSE

To give children the opportunity to deduce principles governing a grammatical feature by comparing two texts containing different facets of the same feature.

## RESOURCES

Two versions of the same text illustrating the feature of the lesson, eg one in the present tense, the other in the past tense.

## INSTRUCTIONS

- Tell the children the objective of the lesson and underline/highlight the first example of the difference(s) between the two versions.
- Discuss the differences with the children.
- Highlight and discuss the next two or three examples.
- Where appropriate make a list to categorise the differences, eg past tense can be present tense with **-ed** added (**work**/**worked**) or it can be a different word entirely (**catch**/**caught**).
- Between you, highlight the remaining examples in the text.

## VARIATION

The children have versions of the texts on clipboards (one between two). After you have demonstrated what to do with the first example, let them find the next.

## Cloze

### PURPOSE

To give children the opportunity to consider the effectiveness of a particular word within a sentence and to practise using effective language to suit the audience and purpose of the text.

### RESOURCES

- Page of enlarged text with all the examples of a particular word class obscured with concealing tape.
- Dry-wipe boards, one between two.

### INSTRUCTIONS

- Tell the children the objective of the lesson and point to the first concealed word.
- Ask the children, in pairs, to discuss what word the tape might be obscuring and to write down their suggestion on their dry-wipe boards.
- Discuss alternative suggestions.
- Compare with the original word.
- Encourage divergence of response, eg for later work in poetry, rather than clichés.

### VARIATION

Leave some of the words at the end uncovered so that children have an opportunity to identify examples of the word class.

## Construct

### PURPOSE

To allow children to experiment with sentence structure to reinforce knowledge of word classes and sentence construction.

### RESOURCES

Coloured word/phrase cards to construct the sentence to be focused on in the lesson, one word per child, eg noun-verb-adverb **dogs bark loudly**, or one phrase per child, eg subject-verb-object/complement **The friendly Alsatian is swimming in the lake**.

## INSTRUCTIONS

- Give out cards to children. (Any extra children can be used to monitor the activity and could be given the task of being the scribe and writing down the sentences.)
- Put large pieces of paper and a thick felt tip pen around the room.
- Ask children to get together to make sentences.
- When all are sitting down in their sentence groups, one child from the group (or a scribe) writes the sentence on a large sheet of paper.
- Ask the children to get up again and find different children to reform into new sentences and write them down.
- Repeat once more.
- Choose children to read out the three sentences on the sheets and all check that they are proper sentences and then vote for the most ludicrous sentence of the day. Write this up on a 'ludicrous sentence sheet'. (On the last day of term you can vote for the most ludicrous sentence of the term/year.)

## VARIATION (TEACHER-DIRECTED WHOLE CLASS ACTIVITY)

- Place all the shuffled cards face down in piles, eg subject, verb and object/complement.
- Divide the class into three groups, eg subject, verb, object/complement.
- One child from the first, eg subject, group takes the top strip from their pile and holds it.
- Next a child from the second, eg verb, group joins him and finally a child from the third, eg object, group.
- The children decide whether each sentence describes something which is possible. They then vote for the silliest sentence.

## VARIATION

This activity can also be played with compound and complex sentences, eg Her brother, who was untidily dressed, led the way.

## Improve

### PURPOSE

To give children practice in editing their writing by considering the choices open to them and discussing the merits of alternative words and structures.

### RESOURCES

- A 'first draft' piece of text (possibly from previous year group) which is weak on the specific elements of the chosen teaching objective.
- Dry-wipe boards between two; pens and erasers.

### INSTRUCTIONS

- Ask the children to read through the draft either in unison or silently.
- Explain what aspect(s) of the writing you want the children to focus on, eg over-use of and then, monotonous sentence openings, long-winded constructions.
- Discuss the first instance of the focus element and change accordingly.
- Ask a child to find the next instance.
- Ask the children to suggest alternatives by writing them on their dry-wipe boards.
- Ask the children to hold up their dry-wipe boards, and choose a pair to read out their version.
- Ask the class to discuss the version given.
- Possibly choose another version.
- Decide which version to insert on the draft on the board.
- Continue through the draft.

# UNIT A
# Y2 Term 1 S2, T4 and T11

## OBJECTIVES

**S2** to find examples, in fiction and non-fiction, of words and phrases that link sentences;

**T4** to understand time and sequential relationships in stories, i.e. what happened when;

**T11** to use language of time to structure a sequence of events, e.g. *'when I finished …'*, *'suddenly …'*, *'after that …'*;

## Principles and explanation

● Some words and phrases at the start of sentences help to link or connect sentences together so that sentences follow on from each other in a time sequence, eg **later on**, **suddenly**, **after that**, **finally**, **first**, **next**, **later**, **meanwhile**, **then**, **after a while**, **when I finished**.

● Children often use **and then** to link ideas, which can be boring. To avoid using **and then** start a new sentence, join the sentences or start a new sentence with a connecting word or phrase, eg:
  **They saw the dogs and then they looked at the cows** could become:
  **They saw the dogs. Then they looked at the cows.**
  **After they saw the dogs, they looked at the cows.**
  **They saw the dogs. After that, they looked at the cows.**

● Rereading and retelling of stories helps embed writing structures rather than speech patterns.

## Sentence level activities
### Compare (page 128)

**Version 1**
Jodie went outside and it was sunny and then she sat on the doorstep and waited and then she saw Mrs Bucket going up the street to the shop and then she saw Sandy ride past on his bike and he wobbled so much that Jodie had to laugh and then she saw the postman and then it was Milko visiting each house with one or two pints and then she saw Mrs Bucket come out of the shop and then Jodie saw that Mrs Bucket was struggling with two large shopping bags and then she ran to help.

**Version 2**
Jodie went outside. It was sunny, so she sat on the doorstep and waited. First she saw Mrs Bucket going up the street to the shop. A little later on she saw Sandy ride past on his bike. He wobbled so much that Jodie had to laugh. Next she saw the postman. Later on it was Milko visiting each house with one or two pints. Finally, she saw Mrs Bucket come out of the shop. When Jodie saw that Mrs Bucket was struggling with two large shopping bags she ran to help.

### Collect and classify (page 128)
List the connectives used in version 2 of the Compare activity above. Continue to collect from fiction and non-fiction texts over the next weeks. Make two lists – fiction and non-fiction – and indicate the type of non-fiction text, eg instructions.

### Oral
Use linking words and phrases when carrying out everyday tasks, eg **First, we'll do the register. After that we'll settle down to some work.**

## Improve (page 130)

We walked up Conrays to the fire station and then we saw a fire engine and then we saw the pole they slide down and then they took us outside to look at a fireman put out a real fire and then he had to squirt water over a burning bin and then they gave us biscuits and a glass of orange and then it was over and then we walked back to school and then we had to draw a picture of the engine.

## Cloze (page 129)

Find a text containing connectives linking a sequence of events, eg *Eat Up, Gemma* by Sarah Hayes (Walker Books), *Aesop's Fables* (Usborne Story Books), *Dear Greenpeace* by Simon James (Walker Books), eg:

**The Rules for 'Draw a Snake'.**
Playing 'Draw a snake upon my back' is easy.
**First** you need to find about six people.
**Next** you have to decide who will be 'it'.
**After that** everyone else lines up against the school wall.
**Meanwhile** 'it' has to think of a pop group or singer.
**Then** 'it' closes her eyes.
**Once** she has her eyes closed everyone else creeps up on her.
**While this is happening** 'it' can turn round and send you back to the wall if she sees you moving.
**After that** whoever draws a snake on 'its' back can have 3 questions to find out about the pop group.
**Then** the questioner makes a guess.
**Finally**, if she is right she swaps places and becomes 'it'.

Cover the connectives with concealing tape.

*Ensure children apply this sentence level learning in their writing.*

## Shared writing

**Related text level objectives:** Y2 Term 1 T4, T10, T11

Plan a simple story on a flow chart. Put in the key temporal connectives, beside the main events. Demonstrate how to convert this into fluent narrative.

> My story begins **Early one morning...**
> Now the next event on my plan is for the girl to go home. I'm going to use the phrase 'Later that evening' to show when this happened: **Later that evening Sehar reached home.** I need a full stop there. She must have been feeling tired so I need to write that. **She was so tired that she slumped down on her bed.** Now she is going to fall asleep so I need to suggest how quickly that happens. **No sooner had her head touched the pillow than Sehar was fast asleep ...** Let's reread that to see if it flows along ...

Stop at appropriate points and give the children two minutes to compose the next sentence (including linking word/phrase) on their dry-wipe boards.

# UNIT B
# Y2 Term 1 S4 (Y2 Term 2 S3 and S4; Y2 Term 3 S2)

## OBJECTIVES

**Y2 Term 1 S4**  to re-read own writing for sense and punctuation;
**Y2 Term 2 S4**  to be aware of grammatical agreement in speech and writing;

## Principles and explanation

- Children have to consider so many different elements, eg spelling, handwriting, content, when they write, that they often 'lose track' in the course of writing. They should be encouraged to rehearse each sentence before committing it to paper, read it back after they have written it and read 'from the top' every so often to ensure there is cohesion in the writing.
- Writing for a genuine audience and/or 'publishing' work in scrap-books, anthologies, etc., helps children see the need to 'get it right'.
- The form of a verb changes according to its subject, eg I want, he wants. This is more obvious in the verb to be – I am/he is/they are, I was/you were. There are variations between many spoken dialects and written standard English.
- The most common construction of the simple sentence is subject/verb/object (SVO), eg the dog (subject) digs (verb) a hole (object) or subject/verb/complement (SVC) the dog (subject) is (verb) tired (complement).

## Sentence level activities

### Construct (page 129)

The children should first pair up red and green cards and then go off to find a child with a blue card which makes a sentence when placed between them in the order: green – blue – red, eg He is happy (not He are happy).

| SUBJECT CARDS (EG GREEN) | VERB CARDS (EG BLUE) | COMPLEMENT CARDS (EG RED) |
|---|---|---|
| You | were | happy |
| She | were | sad |
| He | was | little |
| We | was | friendly |
| They | was | jolly |
| Her friend | is | busy |
| The teacher | is | tidy |
| The doctor | is | helpful |
| Mrs Bloggs | are | tired |
| We | are | bossy |

## Missing verbs

Give children fans (one between two) on which verbs are written. Say the subject and object of a sentence, eg **They bread** and ask the children to find a suitable verb on the fan to fill the space, eg **sell**.

| VERBS FOR FANS | SUBJECT-OBJECT | | SUBJECT-OBJECT | |
|---|---|---|---|---|
| digs | They | the baby. | I | the dishes |
| wash | I | houses. | They | football. |
| makes | He | a noise. | It | holes. |
| sell | She | curry. | He | the windows. |
| plays | We | cars. | They | bread. |
| build | She | the violin. | We | the bath. |
| | He | the garden. | She | potatoes. |
| | It | the dinner. | It | pies. |
| | I | clothes. | We | sandcastles. |

*Ensure children apply this sentence level learning in their writing.*

## Shared writing

**Related text level objectives:** Y2 Term 2 T13, T14; Y2 Term 3 T10–T12, T20, T21

- Remind the children:
    - *Before they write*, to think through (rehearse) sentences to check that they make sense.
    - *As they write*, to keep rereading to make sure that their sentences flow.
    - *After they have written*, to reread their work to check that it makes sense, that it cannot be improved and that it is accurate.

- At points during shared writing ask the children to decide what to write next and to write it down on dry-wipe boards. Check the dry-wipe boards for accurate sentences, with agreement correct. Alternatively, write down the next sentence on the white board with incorrect agreement. Ask the children to rewrite the sentence on their dry-wipe boards accurately.

# UNIT C
# Y2 Term 1 S5 and S6

## OBJECTIVES

**S5** to revise knowledge about other uses of capitalisation, e.g. for names, headings, titles, emphasis, and begin to use in own writing;

**S6** to use a variety of simple organisational devices, e.g. arrows, lines, boxes, keys, to indicate sequences and relationships;

## Principles and explanation

● Capital letters are used for the first letter of a sentence; for 'I'; for special names such as people, places, titles, headings, days of the week, months, planets, organisations; for people's initials; sometimes for abbreviations; for emphasis; for important words in the titles of books, films, etc.; sometimes for the first line in a poem, etc.

● Link this closely to writing in sentences. It is an objective to return to on many occasions, formally and informally, so that over time starting a sentence with a capital letter becomes a habit.

● Instructional and explanatory texts, in particular, employ devices such as arrows, lines, boxes, etc. for clarity and often brevity.

## Sentence level activities

### Collect and classify (page 128)

Look for capital letters on a page from three or four different sorts of books. Classify them according to their function – beginning of a sentence, names (people, places, days, months), personal pronoun 'I', first lines of poem, titles, initials, other. Add to the list in subsequent days as more examples are found. Make a poster as a reminder when writing.

### Spot the capital

Read a paragraph from a book or other text such as a travel brochure in which there are quite a few names, names of places, days of week, months. The children should not be able to see it. When you read a word which starts with a capital, children should raise their hands and say 'capital'. When you finish a sentence, say 'full stop'. Display the text afterwards.

 Sally Bucket lived in Busky Lane near to the Spa shop. She knew that she also lived in Liverpool but that was a big place. She lived in a row of houses like a giant loaf of bread. Each house was joined to the next one. Sally thought that if the end house got pushed too hard by the wind they might all fall over. She had seen her uncle Ned do that with cards.

In Busky Lane lived Sally's friends. There was her best friend Sita. There were Kylie and Jason. They lived at number 28. They were twins and had their birthday on the same day in June. Sally's birthday was in April. Sita's birthday was in December. It was like having two Christmases at once. Sally also had a brother who was a bit of a bother. His name was Billy Bucket.

Today was Wednesday. Sally was very excited. On Monday Sita's mum had promised to take both the girls out on Wednesday. Today was Wednesday so Sally waited at the window looking out for Sita.

*Ensure children apply this sentence level learning in their writing.*

## Shared writing

**Related text level objectives:** Y2 Term 1 T13–T18

● Describe how to get from the school to a nearby point which requires using names of streets, towns, etc. as appropriate. Use connectives, eg **To Medwell station. Walk out of the front gate. Next, turn left down Angel Rd. Then cross the street at the lights at Waller's chemist.**

> Let's start with the title: **To Medwell station**.
> That will need a capital at the beginning. Does it need any further capitals? **To Medwell station**, yes, of course Medwell is a name. Instruction number 1 **Walk out of the front gate**. Capital letter for walk as it's the start of the sentence and of course a full stop at the end, etc.

After writing the title and the two opening instructions, ask the children where to go after that. Consider a suitable connective and where the capital letters belong. Notice the direct language: **walk, turn, cross** – no unnecessary words.

If the destination is not reached before the end of the lesson, this activity can be concluded in independent time. Discuss the merits of instructions as opposed to a map. The children could draw a map in independent time putting in street names with capital letters (including Rd., St., Ave., Close).

● During all shared writing, emphasise and talk aloud about the need to use and check for capital letters, especially at the start of sentences, for names and headings. This needs to become an automatic habit, especially for beginning sentences, so it must be emphasised. Sometimes, make purposeful errors by missing out a capital and encourage children to spot when you make an omission.

● Construct and label a flow chart or set of diagrams to perform a classroom task such as washing the paint equipment, feeding an animal, watering plants, turning on the computer.

# UNIT D
# Y2 Term 2 S5, Y2 Term 3 S3

## OBJECTIVE

**S5**  to use verb tenses with increasing accuracy in speaking and writing, e.g. *catch/caught*, *see/saw*, *go/went*; to use past tense for narration;

## Principles and explanation

- Most texts are consistent in their use of tense – generally past or present.
- Certain text types are usually in the past (narrative/recount), some are in the present (instructions, explanations, reports).
- Writing should not move from one tense to another without a reason. Writing should use the standard form and spelling of past tense verbs, which may be different from some people's spoken versions. Use the terms 'standard' and 'non-standard' rather than 'correct' and 'incorrect'.

## Sentence level activities

### Compare (page 128)

My Mum is never, ever late and yet here I am, waiting. Just my luck. I can see the cars outside and I am hopeful that soon Mum's little red car will arrive. I want to go home. I can do what I like at home but sitting here is just a waste of time. When I catch my Mum she is going to be in trouble. TROUBLE is my middle name. Boy, she is in big trouble with me, right now.

My Mum was never, ever late and yet there I was, waiting. Just my luck. I could see the cars outside and I was hopeful that soon Mum's little red car would arrive. I wanted to go home. I could do what I liked at home but sitting there was just a waste of time. When I caught my Mum she was going to be in trouble. TROUBLE was my middle name. Boy, she was in big trouble with me, right then.

### Collect and classify (page 128)

Classify the verbs in the Compare activity into those which end in **-ed** and those which do not. Continue to collect verbs in reading to add to each list.

### Convert

Say some words, eg catch, go, see, ask, play, sleep, read, and ask children to write the past tense version on their dry-wipe boards. Provide a sentence in past/present tense. Pupils write next sentence in same tense.

### Standard

Build a list directly from the children's work (do not reveal sources) of non-standard forms of verbs in past tense, eg He goed away. Provide standard versions. Use for the children to check their own work. The children take it in turns during shared writing to spot either inconsistent use of tense or non-standard forms.

### Oral

Ask children to relate briefly an incident that happened to them. Ask the class to listen out for the past tense verbs and write as many as they can on their dry-wipe boards. Check that the narrator does not veer away from the past tense.

**Improve (page 130)**

The small tortoiseshell butterfly is one of the most common butterflies found in the British Isles. Tortoiseshells come into gardens to feed and will sit, sunbathing on spring flowers. You can see small tortoiseshell butterflies in March or April, if it is warm enough and you have sharp enough eyes.

The caterpillars are green and black. They had little spikes on them. They fed on stinging nettles in spring and during the summer. They lived together in a small bundle of silken threads. You found these beautiful butterflies all over Europe. They were quite easy to keep and hatched out in a classroom. Once they had hatched you should release them. They liked a small patch of nettles in your garden.

*Ensure children apply this sentence level learning in their writing.*

## Shared writing

**Related text level objective:** Y2 Term 2 T13

● When modelling writing, maintain a consistent use of tense, making occasional deliberate mistakes but correcting when you reread.

● Provide a few sentences, shifting tense incorrectly. Alter, as you write.

● Then move on to modelling longer pieces, ensuring consistency. Try out sentences in the past and present tenses to see which it should be.

> **Sly was a cunning fox. He stared at the chicken. The chicken looks back at him.** No, that sounds odd. Which word sounds odd. Let's reread it. … Yes the word **looks** sounds odd. It should be **looked. The chicken looked back at him.** That is better. Now, I want to bring the farmer out to catch Sly. But first I want to show how Sly is feeling hungry and the chicken is feeling scared. I know, what about this – **Sly felt his stomach rumble. The chicken feels his knees tremble.** Does that sound right? No, I've changed tense again. Let's put that right.

> Now, in my next sentence I am going to have the farmer come out of his house. On your dry-wipe boards write down the next sentence. Start with the words **The farmer** … and make sure you use the right tense. Reread what I have written and make sure that your sentence follows on properly.

# UNIT E
# Y2 Term 2 S6

## OBJECTIVE

**S6** to identify speech marks in reading, understand their purpose, use the terms correctly;

## Principles and explanation

Speech marks enclose what is actually being said. The speech marks demarcate the beginning and end of what is being said. You can use a character's 'voice' to bring their speech alive. (The actual use of speech marks does not become an objective until Year 3 Term 1, though by then many children will already be using them.)

## Sentence level activities

### Identify

- Identify who speaks in a text, highlighting what they say. Read aloud with expression.
- Using a known text, examine where speech marks are positioned and decide what they are for. Check in other texts, eg *Hue Boy* by Rita Phillips Mitchell (Gollancz).

### Match

Match card strips of speech enclosed by speech marks (**'I want butter on my bread!'**) with strips stating who spoke (**the king roared**).

*Ensure children apply this sentence level learning in their writing.*

## Shared writing

**Related text level objectives:** Y2 Term 2 T6

- Relate direct speech to work on character. Collect what a character says that shows the sort of person they are – their feelings and motives. Invent what the character might say next, given how they are feeling and what has happened to them. During shared writing keep stopping to point out what the character is like and therefore what sort of thing they might say or do. Comment in reading on different possible responses from characters in contrast to what is said or done. It is helpful to act out how characters speak and act, even if very briefly.

> Now this is what she actually said, so I need to use speech marks at the beginning … and now I need speech marks at the end to show that she has stopped speaking. Let's read it aloud and I'll use a voice for the angry Queen, to show what she said. I've written **she said** – is there a better word instead of **said** to show that she felt angry? What else could we use? OK, we could say **she roared**, **she screamed**, **she yelled** or **she snapped**. Which do you think the Queen would have done?

- Ask the children to write using speech bubbles and then 'burst the bubble' so only the shreds are left (the speech marks and punctuation).

# UNIT F
# Y2 Term 2 S7

## OBJECTIVE

**S7**   to investigate and recognise a range of other ways of presenting texts, e.g. speech bubbles, enlarged, bold or italicised print, captions, headings and sub-headings;

## Principles and explanation

There are many different ways to present and organise texts to help the reader.  A range of different devices is used by writers with the intention of helping the reader, for instance by drawing attention to certain key aspects of a text or presenting information in an easily accessible way. It is easy for adults to take presentational devices and text conventions for granted. Help children to notice not just the meaning of texts, but the ways authors, designers and publishers draw attention to that meaning.

## Sentence level activities

- Show the children a page in which certain devices such as bold, capitalisation, italic have been used. Discuss why the author has chosen to use them.
- Give out a number of texts for the children to look through in groups to find more. They should consider why they are used and be prepared to tell the class.
- Under headings (bold, all caps, italic, underlined, enlarged, 'other') classify the examples to see whether authors follow similar conventions.
- Examine some non-fiction texts to ascertain how authors use headings, sub-headings, captions.
- The children survey different texts, including magazines, newspapers, comics. Cut out different features.
- Investigate the use of different typefaces in a non-fiction book, eg for headings, captions, index, glossary.
- Return to a book you have just read with the class, and 'read' it again for organisational and presentational devices: 'How did the author (and designer) help us to read this the way they wanted us to read?'
- Look at dictionaries and glossaries to see different ways to present information. (T16, 17, 18).
- Look at flow charts and diagrams (T19) as examples of different ways to present information. Discuss whether flow charts and diagrams can put messages across more clearly than prose.

*Ensure children apply this sentence level learning in their writing.*

## Shared writing

**Related text level objectives:** T13–T15, T20

In shared writing use such devices as bold, enlarged and italicised print sparingly otherwise children may overuse such devices. Speech bubbles can be used in other curriculum areas to capture key questions for investigations or key comments and observations made by different children, eg writing up observations in science. Headings and sub-headings are increasingly useful in non-fiction as they help children separate and organise information into distinctive paragraphs.

If possible, conduct shared writing sessions using ICT facilities, demonstrating the use of italic and bold print, etc.

# UNIT G
# Y2 Term 2 S8 (Y2 Term 3 S4)

## OBJECTIVE

**S8**   to use commas to separate items in a list;

## Principles and explanation

- Before dealing with lists, take the opportunity to look at the word class of nouns. A noun is a word that denotes somebody or something. In the sentence **My younger sister won some money in a competition**, **sister**, **money** and **competition** are nouns.
- Proper nouns are the names of people, places, organisations, days of the week, months, seasons, etc. These normally begin with a capital letter, eg **Amanda**, **Birmingham**, **Microsoft**, **November**.
- When writing lists, commas are used between each item except the last one preceding the word **and**. To help children avoid inserting commas at every opportunity teach them the test of asking themselves, 'Is this a list?'

## Sentence level activities

### Label

Spend some time labelling items, by naming them, around the room.

### Nouns

Write a sentence on the board and underline the nouns in a bright colour, eg **The dog ate the doughnut**. Ask the children to identify the two nouns in the sentence. Now, move on to a number of sentences where the nouns are obvious. Notice that the words **the**, **a** or **an** are usually before the noun. Notice that you could add in another word to describe, or give more information about, a noun. Make lists of nouns from around the room, in a kitchen, on a farm, in the market, in a toy shop, etc.

### Function (page 128)

Choose a text containing a number of nouns, eg *Letters from Lucy* by Moira Andrew, illustrated by Rhian Nest James (Collins Educational). The non-noun in this example is in *italics*.

Milk does not just come from a shop. It comes from cows and this is how. Cows eat grass in the summer and silage or hay in the winter. Cows go on making milk for quite a long time after their calves are born. Twice a day the cows are milked by a machine. The machine is run by electricity and has four tubes which attach to the cow's udder. The machine sucks the milk from the cow. This goes along pipes into a large container which cools it down. A refrigerated tanker collects the milk from the farm usually twice a day and takes the milk to a processing-plant where it is put into bottles or cartons. Still refrigerated, it is *taken* to shops and supermarkets to be sold.

### I went to market

- Play the cumulative game 'I went to market and I bought …'. Each child repeats the list of items bought so far, and adds a new item, eg **I went to market and I bought a horse, a Play Station, some carrots and a banana.**

- After about seven or eight items, write the sentence up on the board, without commas. Explain that all the items are **nouns**. Read without commas and ask children if there is anything we can do to make it less of a jumble.
- Provide small pieces of Blu-tak which can be moulded to comma shapes, and ask children to put commas in the right places to separate the items in the list. Discuss whether you need one before **and**.

## Collect and classify 1 (page 128)

Display a text which contains a number of lists – sometimes long, sometimes just two items – and some phrases. Highlight all the commas and all instances of the word **and**. Classify the lists into *two items* and *three or more items*. Rather than write out the lists, draw brackets round them and write 2 or 3+ above each list as shown.

|           2            |            2            |                3+                 |
| :--: | :--: | :--: |

[My brother and I] went off to buy some [fish and chips]. On the way we met [Sarah, Anna and

                      **3+**

Spud]. They told us they were going to buy [some fish for the cat, some hay for the horse, some

pellets for the chickens and some chips for themselves]. So we all strolled along together – [Sarah,

     **3+**

Anna, Spud, my brother and I]. Now I am not a coward but as soon as I saw the old man coming

      **3+**

towards us I felt afraid. He had a dog with him. It was not [a friendly retriever, a perky pekinese or a

silly spaniel]. It looked like a wolf. We did not wait around to check if it was friendly. We ran [past

     **3+**

the chip shop, down Creedys, across the pitch, up by the supermarket and into Marley's Lane].

There we stopped …

## Collect and classify 2 (page 128)

Skim a variety of texts to collect examples of commas in lists, eg *The Very Hungry Caterpillar* by Eric Carle (Penguin); *Don't Forget the Bacon* by Pat Hutchins (Puffin); *Hue Boy* by Rita Phillips Mitchell (Gollancz); *Winnie the Witch* by Korky Paul and Valerie Thomas (OUP); *The Elephant and the Bad Baby* by Elfrida Vipont (Puffin). Derive principles about using commas in lists and display one or two examples on a poster as a reminder.

*Ensure children apply this sentence level learning in their writing.*

## Shared writing

**Related text level objectives:** Y2 Term 2 T13, T15; Y2 Term 3 T10, T20, T21

- Write a section from the traditional tale, eg in which Little Red Riding Hood fills a basket with a number of items.
- Write pretend ingredients for a school outing, a birthday party, or a summer holiday, etc. **You need soft sand, a sun as hot as chillis, lots of pebbles, the cool waves, rock pools, crabs and an ice cream.**
- Write a list poem.

# UNIT H
# Y2 Term 2 S9 (Y2 Term 3 S5)

## OBJECTIVE

**S9**   to secure the use of simple sentences in own writing;

## Principles and explanation

Defining a sentence to young children must be in the simplest of terms, eg sentences must make sense and be complete on their own. Sentences begin with a capital letter and end with a full stop (or question or exclamation mark). Children acquire the concept of a sentence almost certainly through immersion in the language of books and usage rather than explanation.

*Note:* The text in some picture books uses oral language structures and the effects of a story teller; sometimes text demarcated by a full stop is not a sentence, eg 'A big branch for Sarah, a small branch for Percy, and an old bit of ivy for Bill.' (*Owl Babies*).

## Sentence level activities

### Read

With any shared text, take a few minutes to look at the sentences, identifying them by full stop and capital letter. Read some amusing or otherwise notable ones out and encourage the children to memorise and mimic them.

### Fix it

Rewrite a few sentences of text from a book without the punctuation. (Choose a text which has some short and some slightly longer sentences, but no commas.) Read it through in one breath and gasp at the end. Put full stops at even intervals through the text as places for breathing (possibly at the end of each line). Read it again. Discuss the fact that full stops are not merely places to breathe; they enable the reader to make sense of the text. Ask the children whether the text consists of sentences even though there are no full stops. Discuss the fact that sentences are self-contained units of meaning.

the golden eagle is the largest bird to be found in the British Isles golden eagles are found mainly in the scottish highlands some people confuse the eagle with the buzzard the buzzard is much smaller the eagle has a strong flight it has a square white tail which ends in a broad black band there are streaks of white under the wings the hooked beak makes the eagle look fierce the golden eagle can kill a weak lamb and carry it off to its nest they are very large birds they are also very beautiful

### Compare 1 (page 128)

Discuss the differences between labels or titles (of books, pictures, songs or poems) and sentences.

| LABELS/TITLES | SENTENCES |
| --- | --- |
| The frosty morning in the park | The morning was frosty in the park. |
| Julie on the swings | Julie was on the swings. |
| Playing on the swings | Julie is playing on the swings. |
| Mrs Jones | Her name is Mrs Jones. |
| Shopping at the supermarket | Mrs Jones is shopping at the supermarket. |

## Sentences

- Send two children out of the room. Ask the rest of the children questions about a character in a book they know, eg 'What did Plop look like? Where did he live? Who looked after him? Why was he afraid of the dark?' Encourage quick, 2- or 3-word, answers for you to write on the board.
- Ask the two to come back in and read the information (the answers you have just written on the board). Ask them if it makes sense, whether they can understand it, and if not, why? Then ask the rest of the children to formulate complete pieces of information, ie sentences.
- Point out that in conversations, answers to questions are usually one or two words. They are very rarely sentences and that on their own they make no sense. When you give information as the answer of a question in writing, the answer must incorporate information from the question and in so doing it becomes a sentence.

## Construct (page 129)

| BEGINNINGS (SUBJECT) (BLUE) | ENDINGS  (RED) |
|---|---|
| The dog | swam in the sea. |
| The fish | ran down the road. |
| Tom | wrote a good story. |
| The baby | couldn't turn the tap off. |
| The air hostess | slept in a nest. |
| Mum | mended roads. |
| The dentist | parked the car on a yellow line. |
| My teacher | sang in the bath. |
| Our hamster | ate worms. |
| That man | painted the chair red. |
| The singer | didn't like figs. |
| A painter | couldn't blow bubbles. |
| A bird | made bread. |
| This little poodle | fed the penguins. |

### VARIATION

Give out equal numbers of subject and **and** cards and double the number of endings cards (eg seven subject cards, seven **and** cards and fourteen endings cards). The children should make sentences using one subject, **and,** and two endings. These are compound sentences.

### Sort out

Extract sentences from a favourite picture book and put on to card strips. Cut up into individual words. Children make up own sentences.

### Compare 2 (page 128)

Compare a text that has full stops and one that does not. Read through both. Which is easy to read and why?

### Collect

Read and underline/circle/highlight sentences in a passage.

### Extending sentences

On strips, provide sentence + conjunction, eg **Liam picked up the key but** …. The children have to complete the sentences.

### Deciding

Select from a list, sentences and non-sentences. Discuss why some are not sentences (verb is missing, incomplete).

*Ensure children apply this sentence level learning in their writing.*

## Shared writing

**Related text level objectives:** Y2 Term 2 T13–T15; Y2 Term 3 T10

● Remind the children that during any writing, they should:
  – rehearse each sentence orally before writing it down;
  – think about whether it needs embellishing or varying;
  – check it makes sense and is complete;
  – start with a capital letter and end with a full stop, question mark or exclamation mark;
  – get into the habit of getting it right first time.

● In shared writing demonstrate several lines yourself, then create several with the whole class and finally move into creating ideas on dry-wipe boards. Some pupils find it helpful to list briefly possible subjects for sentences before independent writing.

> **The old woman struggled through the tall grass.** I need a full stop there and a capital letter. For the next sentence, instead of repeating **the old woman**, I'll use **she**. How about **She was lost.**? That makes sense but it needs more detail. I know: **She had not gone far when she realised that she was lost.** I'll just reread that to see how it sounds…

- Provide opening words for children to complete sentences in pairs, eg She ..., The angry dog .... Provide other openings, such as an adverbial phrase, eg Last week ..., First of all ....

## Notes

- Set 'using capital letters/full stops' as a target; mark for it specifically.
- Some children who struggle may find it useful to put a small tick at the bottom of the page every time they use a capital letter and full stop. This helps to draw their attention to demarcating sentences.
- Use children's own work to demonstrate how to demarcate sentences. Isolate examples in children's own work for them to revisit and correct.
- Pull together groups of children who struggle with the concept of a sentence for a guided session, to revisit work from previous terms.
- Write a variety of list poems where each idea is a sentence. Use a repeating phrase to make this easy. Emphasise the importance of capital letter and full stop as an automatic habit. Use the writing as a chance to develop the embellishment of ideas and use of a range of adventurous vocabulary. For instance, the following opening lines can be used to emphasise sentence structure within a creative activity:

I am afraid of …
I wish I was …
It's a secret but …
I dreamed I saw …
That was the day when …
I'm quiet when …/I'm noisy when …
Here is a …
I looked through the window of dreams and saw …
In my head there is a …
I may be small but …
It was so quiet that I heard …

# UNIT I
# Y2 Term 3 S6 and S7

## OBJECTIVES

**S6** to turn statements into questions, learning a range of 'wh' words typically used to open questions – *what*, *where*, *when*, *who*; to add question marks;

**S7** to compare a variety of forms of question from texts, e.g. *asking for help*, *asking the time*, *asking someone to be quiet*;

## Principles and explanation

- Questions are sentences that are usually meant to gain a response. They may be asked to seek information, ask permission or help or as a polite demand, eg **Could you be quiet?**
- Some questions begin with question words such as **who, what, why, where, when.**
- Some questions are statements with the words reordered, eg **Has he got a pair of scissors? Is she better? Can you play the piano?**
- Questions asking permission and for help, and polite commands often start: **Please may …?, Could …?, Would it be possible …?**

## Sentence level activities

- Write a statement and below it the same statement turned into a question, eg **Jill ran down the road. Why did Jill run down the road?**
- List differences, eg question mark; different word order; change of spelling to verb; use of **did** and question word **why**; the first sentence tells you something, the second asks you something and needs a reply, etc.
- List the sorts of questions children ask in the classroom, eg **Can we go out to play?** and typical questions asked at home, eg **Have you tidied your room?**
- Draw children's attention to your own questions – and theirs. Discuss which type of question they are.
- Collect questions into two sorts: information and permission/help/demand.
- Take statements and change into questions, using question words.
- Sort a list of questions and statements into two piles.
- Collect and list different ways of writing questions.
- Collect and use question openings to stories.
- Use a 'question hand' (on each finger there is a different **wh** word – **who, where, when, what, why**) to generate questions in other subject areas, eg science investigations.
- Use the 'question hand' to plan recounts and narrative: **Who?** – characters; **Where?** – setting; **When** did this occur?; **What** happened?, **Why?** – underlying theme.

*Ensure children apply this sentence level learning in their writing.*

# Shared writing

**Related text level objectives:** Y2 Term 3 T14

- Use work from across the curriculum to generate a list of statements, 'What we know' or 'What we have found out'. Alongside this, list questions under the title, 'What we would like to know'.
- When discussing poetry/narrative, encourage children to ask questions about the text – both the content as well as the way it is written.
- After reading a poem/picture book, discuss what we liked/did not like, and what puzzled us – frame the puzzles as questions to ask the author.
- List what we know about a character and questions we'd ask him/her.
- Rehearse the question sentence, as well as reinforcing the need to use a question mark, eg **Is Bernard naughty?**
- Write a 'who' poem in praise of a friend or relative. This can be an opportunity for exaggeration. For instance:

**Who put a lid on a volcano?**
**It was my best friend James.**


**Who can blow stronger than the North wind?**
**It is my best friend James.**

- Write a 'where' poem. Make this magical. Children can work in pairs – or list questions together and children find answers. Emphasise correct spelling of 'where' and reinforce the need for a question mark. For instance, begin by listing ordinary questions but invent magical answers:

**Where do clouds come from?**
**They are made by the misty breath of the moon-giants.**


**Where does the primrose get its scent?**
**It comes from the yellow tang of a lemon.**

- Invent 'why' poems, eg **Why is it me who does all the tidying?** Alternatively, work in pairs. Each child writes a list of questions using any question starter (**who, why, where, can you,** etc.). The lists of questions are swapped and magical answers written in reply.

# Part 3

## Summary of organisation and language features: fiction and poetry

| TEXT TYPE | PURPOSE | GENERIC TEXT STRUCTURE | SENTENCE/WORD LEVEL FEATURES |
|---|---|---|---|
| Retelling traditional tales | • To entertain and to pass on traditional culture | • Opening that includes a setting (of place and time) and introduces characters<br>• A series of events that build up<br>• Complication(s)<br>• Resulting events<br>• Resolution and ending | • Written in first or third person<br>• Written in past tense<br>• Chronological<br>• Main participants are human or animal contrasting 'good' and 'bad'<br>• Use of motifs, eg principle of three, youngest son as hero<br>• Connectives that signal time, eg early that morning, later on, once<br>• Dialogue in differing tenses<br>• Verbs used to describe actions, thoughts and feelings<br>• Language effects used to create impact on reader, eg adverbs, adjectives, expressive verbs, similes, etc.<br>• Some use of repetitive structures, eg … but the first tasted too hot … but the second tasted too cold |
| Adventure | • To entertain and enthral<br>• To allow escape from reality – the humdrum | • Opening that includes a setting (of place and time) and introduces characters<br>• A series of events that builds up<br>• A complication and series of 'cliffhangers'<br>• Resulting events<br>• Resolution and ending | • Written in first or third person<br>• Written in past tense (occasional use of present)<br>• Chronological; possible use of time shifts<br>• Main participants are human, or animal, contrasting 'good' and 'bad'<br>• Use of stereotypical characters, settings and events, eg nightmares, nightime events, being lost or chased<br>• Connectives that signal time, eg First thing, later that day, early that morning<br>• Connectives used to shift attention, eg meanwhile, at that very moment<br>• Connectives used to inject suspense, eg suddenly, without warning<br>• Dialogue, in differing tenses<br>• Verbs used to describe action, thoughts and feelings<br>• Language effects used to create impact on reader, eg adverbs, adjectives, precise nouns, expressive verbs, metaphors, similes, etc. |
| Free verse | • To entertain<br>• To recreate experience<br>• To create an experience | • Opening and closure<br>• Range of possible structures<br>• Words used to create a varied pattern on the page | Possible use of:<br>• internal rhyme and rhythm<br>• half or near rhyme<br>• alliteration and onomatopoeia<br>• assonance and dissonance<br>• metaphor and simile (personification)<br>• expressive adjectives, adverbs and verbs<br>• unusual word combinations<br>• use of patterns, repetition |
| Haiku | • To entertain<br>• To recreate the essence of natural experience<br>• To capture a profound experience in a few words | • Opening and closure<br>• Three lines | Possible use of:<br>• alliteration, onomatopoeia<br>• assonance/dissonance<br>• metaphoric language<br>• simile<br>• expressive vocabulary<br>• careful use of punctuation to add meaning<br>• unusual word combinations |

## WRITER'S KNOWLEDGE

- Borrow words and phrases to link the tale together.
- Rehearse by constant retelling before writing.
- Be clear about the few key events.
- Add in detail to embellish – but do not add in too much or you may distract the reader from the main events.
- Try to see the story happening in your head as you retell events/write.
- Use some repetitive lines, eg **so he huffed and he puffed** …, especially if you wish the audience to join in.
- Keep the main characters distinctively good, bad, lazy, silly, etc.
- You can alter the setting and many details but the main events in the plot have to stay, eg Snow White in New York.
- Reread the tale aloud to see if it 'reads well'. Try it out on small groups.

- Avoid telling the reader what to feel, eg **it was scary**, but make the reader feel it through concrete description.
- Avoid telling the reader what a character feels, eg **she was sad**, but show how characters feel through what they say or do, eg **her lip trembled**.
- Know your ending so that events can be planned and written that converge at the end – otherwise some irrelevant details will creep in or the story may ramble.
- Do not plan too many characters or you may lose control of them.
- Give your main character some sort of flaw and make him or her interesting.
- Give your character a 'feeling' at the start of the story as this will influence events.
- Keep thinking as you write 'what would this person do/say?'.
- Plan just a few details about the character that tells the reader something about their personality.
- Include the weather, season and time of day as part of creating the setting.
- To create suspense, lull the reader into a false sense of security – get characters doing something pleasant and then introduce a dilemma.
- Use exclamations for impact, eg **Help!**
- Use questions to draw the reader into events, eg Where should they look now?
- At the end, show how the main character has changed as a result of the narrative.
- At the end, have the narrator or a character make comments on what has happened.

- Avoid abstract nouns, such as love, eternity, etc.
- Describe in a concrete way what you think you are writing about.
- Keep rereading to capture flow and rhythm.
- Only use simile if it comes swiftly, otherwise it sounds false.
- Metaphor is more powerful than simile.
- Use unusual but revealing word combinations to surprise the reader.
- Play with words and ideas.
- Hold the subject in your mind as you write.
- Observe very carefully the details of your subject.
- Use your senses.
- Select words which are linked to the senses, eg **click, crack, greasy, jagged**.
- Write very quickly in a totally focused way.
- Write about subjects that you know a lot about and that matter.
- Have the subject in front of you so you can observe it.
- Use the shape on the page to emphasise words and ideas.
- Avoid clichés.
- Read aloud to hear how it sounds.
- Be ruthless in revision so that each word is fresh and each word counts.

- Use careful observation of events and scenes.
- Create a verbal 'snapshot' to capture precisely the essence of a moment.
- Possibly focus on a seemingly insignificant detail that suggests more than it states.
- Use a few words to evoke more than is described, eg suggesting the season.
- Use language to capture a sense of wonder or surprise about simple things.
- Select one or two details only.
- Use a 'sound effect' to emphasise loneliness or isolation.
- Begin by making notes outside of small details.
- Try to use words to help the reader see something familiar in a new light.

# Summary of organisation and language features: non-fiction

| TEXT TYPE | PURPOSE | GENERIC TEXT STRUCTURE | SENTENCE/WORD LEVEL FEATURES |
|---|---|---|---|
| Recount | • To retell events | • Orientation – scene setting opening, eg I went to the shop …<br>• Events – recount of the events as they occurred, eg I saw a vase …<br>• Reorientation – a closing statement, eg When I got back, I told my mum. (with elaboration in more sophisticated texts) | • Written in the past tense, eg I went<br>• In chronological order, using connectives that signal time, then, next, after, meanw…<br>• Focus on individual or group participants, eg we, I |
| Non-chronological report | • To describe the way things are | • An opening, general classification, eg Sparrows are birds.<br>• More technical classification (optional), eg Their Latin name is …<br>• A description of the phenomenon, including some or all of its:<br>  – qualities, eg Birds have feathers.<br>  – parts and their function, eg The beak is …<br>  – habits/behaviour or uses, eg They nest in … | • Written in the present tense they nest<br>• Non-chronological<br>• Initial focus on generic participants, eg sparrows in general, not Sam the sparro…<br>• Moves from the general to t… specific |
| Instructions and procedures | • To describe (or instruct) how something is done through a series of sequenced steps | • Goal – a statement of what is to be achieved, eg How to make a sponge cake<br>• Materials/equipment needed, listed in order, eg 2 eggs, flour<br>• Sequenced steps to achieve the goal, eg Cream the sugar and butter.<br>• Often diagrams or illustrations | • Written in the imperative, eg Sift the flour<br>• In chronological order, eg fi… next<br>• Use of numbers, alphabet o… bullet points and colour to signal order<br>• Focus on the generalised human agents rather than named individuals. |
| Explanation | • To explain the processes involved in natural and social phenomena, or to explain how something works | • General statement to introduce the topic, eg In the autumn some birds migrate.<br>• A series of logical steps explaining how or why something occurs, eg Because hours of daylight shorten …<br>• Steps continue until the final state is produced or the explanation is complete | • Written in simple present tense, eg Many birds fly south.<br>• Uses connectives that signa… time, eg then, next, sever… months later<br>• Uses causal connectives, e… because, so, this causes |
| Persuasion | • To argue the case for a point of view<br>• To attempt to convince the reader | • Thesis – an opening statement, eg Vegetables are good for you.<br>• Arguments – often in the form of point plus elaboration, eg They contain vitamins. Vitamin C is vital for …<br>• Reiteration – summary and restatement of the opening position, eg We have seen that … so … | • Simple present tense<br>• Focus mainly on generic participants, eg vegetables, a particular vegetable<br>• Mainly logical, rather than connectives which signal ti… eg this shows, however, because<br>• Movement usually from the generic to the specific |
| Discussion | • To present arguments and information from differing viewpoints | • Statement of the issue plus a preview of the main arguments<br>• Arguments for, plus supporting evidence<br>• Arguments against, plus supporting evidence (alternatively, argument/counter argument, one point at a time)<br>• Recommendation – summary and conclusion | • Simple present tense<br>• Generic human (or non-hum… participants<br>• Logical connectives, eg therefore, however<br>• Movement is from the gene… to the specific, eg Hunters agree …, Mr Smith, who hunted for many years, . |

## WRITER'S KNOWLEDGE

- Details are vital to bring incidents alive.
- Use specific names of people, places, objects, etc.
- Pick out incidents that will amuse, interest or that in some way are significant.
- You can write as if you were 'telling the story' of what happened.
- Plan by thinking, noting or drawing – when? who? where? what? and why? Use a flow chart to plan the sequence.
- End by commenting on events.

---

- Plan under paragraph headings in note form.
- Use a range of resources to gather information.
- Select facts from a range of sources to interest the reader, eg books CD-ROM, interviews.
- Possible use of a question in the title to intrigue the reader, eg **Yetis – do they exist?**
- Be clear, so that you do not muddle the reader.
- Open by explaining very clearly what you are writing about – take an angle to draw the reader in.
- Use tables, pictures, diagrams to add more information.
- Possibly end by relating the subject to the reader, eg **Many people like whales** ...
- Reports are factual but you could add comments or use questions to draw in the reader.
- Reread as if you knew nothing about the subject to check that you have put the information across successfully.

---

- Before writing instructions be clear about what is needed and what has to be done, in what order.
- Think about your readers. You will need to be very clear about what to do or they will be muddled – if they are young, you may have to avoid technical language or use simple diagrams.
- The title should explain what the instructions are about – using **how to** ... helps, eg **How to play cricket**.
- In your querying you may need to say when the instructions are needed, eg **If your computer breaks down** ..., or for whom it is best suited, eg **Young children may enjoy this game** ....
- Use bullet points, numbers or letters to help the reader.
- Use short clear sentences so the reader does not become muddled.
- Use the end statements to wrap up the writing – evaluate how useful or how much fun this will be.
- Make your writing more friendly by using **you**, or more formal by just giving orders.
- Use adjectives and adverbs only when needed.
- Tantalise the reader, eg **Have you ever been bored – well this game will** ....
- Draw the reader in with some 'selling points', eg **This is a game everyone loves** ....
- Make instructions sound easy, eg **You are only four simple steps away** ....
- Finally, ask yourself whether someone who knows nothing about this could successfully use your instructions.

---

- Decide whether diagrams, charts, illustrations or a flow chart would help to explain.
- Use a title that indicates what you are writing about.
- Using **how** or **why** in the title helps. Try to make the title intrigue the reader, eg **Why do sloths hang about?**
- Use the first paragraph to introduce your subject to the reader.
- Organise the writing and illustrations to explain: what you need, how it works, why it works (cause and effect), when and where it works, and what it is used for.
- Add in extra, interesting information.
- Try to end by relating the subject to the reader.
- If you use specialised terminology, a glossary may be needed.
- Interest the reader with exclamation, eg **Beware – whirlwinds can kill!** Or use questions, eg **Did you know that** ...?
- Draw the reader in, eg **strange as it may seem** ...; **not many people know that** ...,etc.
- Reread your explanation, pretending to know nothing about the subject – is it clear?

---

- Use good reasons and evidence to convince your readers.
- Use facts rather than just persuasive comments.
- You may wish to counter arguments.
- Try to get the reader interested and on your side – appear reasonable!
- Tantalise your readers so that they agree with you.
- Use strong, positive language.
- Short sentences can help to give emphasis.
- Make the reader think that everyone else does this, agrees or that it will make them a better, happier person, eg **Everyone agrees that** ..., **We all know that** ....
- Draw the reader in, eg **At long last** ... **the x you have been waiting for**.
- Be informative, persuasive and sound friendly.
- Alliteration can help to make slogans memorable, eg **Buy British Beef**.
- Use humour as it can get people on your side.
- A picture that tugs at the heart-strings can be more effective than 1,000 words.
- Finally, reread and decide whether you would be persuaded.

---

- You can turn the title into a question, eg **Should we hunt whales?**
- Open by introducing the reader to the discussion – you may need to add why you are debating the issue.
- Try to see the argument from both sides.
- Support your views with reasons and evidence.
- In your conclusion you must give a reason for what you decide.
- If you are trying to present a balanced viewpoint, check you have been fair to both sides.

# Developing handwriting

## Developing gross motor control

- Consolidate the vocabulary of movement by talking about the movements children make, such as going round and round, making curves, springing up and sliding down, making long, slow movements or quick, jumpy movements.
- Show children how to make large movements in the air with their arms, hands and shoulders. For example, fix ribbons on to the end of sticks for the children to swirl in the air. Encourage the use of both sides of the body.
- Let the children make different body shapes/actions in response to music to help them to remember the shapes.

## Developing letter shapes using gross motor movements

- Encourage sky writing with both hands.
- Ask the teaching assistant or a confident child to model the movement with her/his back to the rest of the children while you stand behind the children to check they are all following the movement correctly.
- Let children make patterns in the air or on each other's backs.
- Make a letter shape in the damp sand tray. Each child in the group traces over the shape, going a little deeper each time. The object is to get down to the base of the sand tray without the sides falling in.
- Reinforce the vocabulary of movement, eg the curly caterpillar, the long ladder and the one-armed robot. Talk about the movements as you make them, using a 'patter', eg for the one-armed robot: 'Start at his head and go down to his feet. Bounce back up and go over for his arm.' While this is helpful in the early stages, it is purely to help to establish the movement. A letter movement can be reinforced by asking the children to write the letter with their eyes closed.

## What should I teach about handwriting in the early Foundation Stage?

In order that children can eventually acquire a legible, fluent and fast handwriting style, they need to develop skills including:

- good gross and fine motor control;
- a recognition of pattern;
- a language to talk about shapes and movements;
- the main handwriting movements involved in the three basic letter shapes, as exemplified by: l, c, r.

## What is the difference between gross and fine motor control?

*Gross motor control* is the term used to describe the development of controlled movements of the whole body, or limbs such as the arms or legs. Of particular importance in relation to handwriting is the development of good posture and balance. Children can develop gross motor control through much of the physical development curriculum recommended in the *Curriculum guidance for the Foundation Stage* (QCA 2000). Activities such as dance, football, use of small apparatus, cycling, gripping climbing frames, building with large-scale construction kits, develop gross motor control.

*Fine motor control* is the term used to describe smaller movements, usually of the hand and fingers (or of the feet and toes for children who communicate using touch sensitive pads with their feet). Fine motor control is best developed through activities which involve small-scale movements such as those listed on page 157 and on page 67 of *Curriculum guidance for the Foundation Stage* (QCA 2000). Until children have gained reasonable fine motor control through art and other activities, formal handwriting worksheets are not appropriate. Some teachers find that boys develop fine motor control more slowly than girls.

## What kinds of letter patterns should I teach?

When you introduce patterns for writing to children, it is useful to focus on features which keep recurring in letter formation, eg:

- focus on patterns which build on the three basic letter shapes: *l*, eg the long ladder; *c*, eg the curly caterpillar and *r*, eg the one-armed robot;
- include patterns that move across the body, from left to right;
- use pattern-making for different purposes. Sometimes, allow children to produce the pattern across the entire line. This encourages fluency of movement and helps to emphasise the right to left direction of our writing system. At other times, it may be useful to restrict the number of repetitions to four or five so that the child learns a little about the need to leave spaces between words;
- keep talking about the movements you make in the patterns;
- let the children invent 'sounds' to make as they draw their patterns, eg a bouncing sound as they bounce up from the one-armed robot's feet, a buzzing sound as you draw anti-clockwise spirals, a shsh sound as you make wave patterns, etc.;
- some children find drawing patterns in time to music helpful. Arches can be formed to slow, relaxed music and the tempo can be changed to a marching rhythm and children encouraged to produce angled movements.

### Developing fine motor control

- Let the children make patterns using pegboards.
- Provide sewing and weaving activities.
- Involve the children in chopping and peeling in cooking activities.
- Provide woodworking tools – pliers, screwdrivers, hammers.
- Use finger rhymes, counting fingers, playing with words and sounds, etc.
- Provide small construction toys.
- Structure sand and water play to include sieving, pouring, picking up toys using tools, etc.
- Develop the pincer movement: show the children how to use tweezers to pick up and sort sequins, small beads, etc., sprinkling coloured sand, glitter, salt, etc. on pictures.
- Let the children use paints, finger paints, etc. for making big patterns on different shaped paper, eg fish, balloons, kites. Talk about the patterns they make. Focus on developing the curly caterpillar, long ladder and one-armed robot.
- Let the children strengthen their fingers by using clay, playdough, plasticine, etc., for modelling. They can make letter shapes and patterns using the modelling media.
- Encourage dexterity by asking the children to cut out large letter shapes or patterns. They can use different coloured marker pens for tracing along inside the shapes. Emphasise that circles and curly caterpillars need to be traced from the top and anti-clockwise.
- Let the children use thick paint brushes and water to paint patterns on walls, fences, etc.

*Encourage sky writing*

157

## Children's names

Children's names are a useful source of learning for both phonics and handwriting. However, some children who come to school already able to write their names may associate the wrong movement with certain letters (the common error is forming o and a using a clockwise movement). A sensitive approach is needed here but when the child has learned the correct movement he or she will have acquired over a third of the alphabet! Close home–school links really pay off in this area and a sheet of letters should always be available for parents (see page 164).

*Children's names are a useful source of learning for both phonics and handwriting.*

## Choice of paper

As children begin to write letters, having practised the letter shapes through skywriting and other large-scale activities, provide them with a large piece of paper (turned landscape) with a single line. Lined paper is important because so much about handwriting is to do with the letters' orientation to the line. Line guides are useful for older children.

## When should I introduce handwriting?

Skills for handwriting can be introduced from a very early stage. However, some children with special educational needs may require specific support or provision according to the nature and extent of their needs. Consult local SEN advisory and support services for guidance on approaches and resources. Offer activities which encourage children to develop controlled movements – both in terms of fine and gross motor control – through all kinds of play and cross-curricular opportunities. Children should be allowed to pick up the writing implement themselves and decide which hand they prefer. Only then should they be given help with the pencil hold (see sections on pencil grip and left-handed children). As children begin to discover their preferred hand for holding a pencil and once they are confidently using flowing movements, they can be introduced to smaller, more controlled activities. Through these, you can reinforce left → right hand movements, moving from the top tc the bottom of a letter and reinforcing the anti-clockwise movement, etc. Some children's previous experience of print forms in languages other than English may have prepared them for the movements required to write English letters. Other children will need to learn there are differences in the directionality of English and other print systems. Specific advice and guidance can be obtained from local ethnic minority achievement services.

## Is there a recommended style of handwriting?

Each school should have a handwriting policy which aims to teach children to write in a way that is legible, fluent and fast. This entails a style which enables the letters to be joined easily. If children find the physical act of scribing taxing, they will be unlikely to develop into confident effective writers. Continuity from Foundation Stage through Key Stages 1 and 2 is vitally important. Not only should a school have an agreed style, but also an agreed 'patter' for helping children to recall the required movement for each letter. Teaching assistants and student teachers should be aware of the style and the 'patter'.

## When should I begin to link letter shapes with sounds?

In early Foundation Stage, while children are working at step 1 of *Progression in phonics* (learning to listen to, and discriminate between, sounds in their environment, in music and in rhyme) they will also be developing the three basic handwriting movements using gross and fine motor control.

Once they move to step 2 of *Progression in phonics* (hearing consonant phonemes in initial position), they will need to learn the letter shapes alongside the letter sound, making use of the kinaesthetic channel (proprioception) to help them to internalise the letter shapes that go with the sounds. Sky writing, writing with paint and marker pens and other large-scale activities are still most appropriate as children learn to associate shapes with letter sounds. Step 2 in *Progression in phonics* introduces 6 letters: s, m, c, t, g, h. All of the letter movements are represented in these groups of letters:

c: c, g, (s)

l: t

r: m, h

## Using 'shape families' for teaching letter formation

For simplicity, the letters of the alphabet can be sorted into four main movement groups. Some letters have different forms – b, ʙ, k, ʀ, y, ɣ, v, ʋ – and so these fall into two groups. Some letters, eg ƒ, s, have some affinity with a group but could be taught separately.

The advantage of aligning letters with a key letter is to help children to remember the starting point and subsequent movement of the letter. This is particularly effective in discriminating b from d.

The four groups are:

- down and off in another direction, exemplified by the letter l (**long ladder**): letters ʙ, i, j, l, t, u (v, w with rounded bases);
- down and retrace upwards, exemplified by the letter r (**one-armed robot**): letters b, h, k, m, n, p, r; (numbers 2, 3, 5 follow a clockwise direction);
- anti-clockwise round, exemplified by the letter c (**curly caterpillar**): letters c, a, d, e, g, o, q, ƒ, s; numbers: 0, 6, 8, 9;
- zigzag letters: letters: (k) v, w, x, y, z; numbers: 1, 4, 7.

### Preventing a confusion between the letters 'b' and 'd'

Introduce each letter of the alphabet in association with its key letter (l, c or r). The letter d is a 'curly caterpillar' letter. It starts exactly like a c but then 'goes up to the top in a straight line and then down again'. The letter b is a 'one-armed robot' letter. It starts higher than the letter r but when it touches the line it goes back again, over and round. In this way children learn letters as movement rather than visual shapes and so they have a mechanism for remembering letters which are visually confusing. In *Progression in phonics*, the letter d is learned in step 3 and the letter b in step 4. If the letters are taught effectively, the motor memory of each letter will be paired with the phoneme and will not present a problem.

*Developing a good posture is as important as developing a good pencil grip.*

*Paper position for right-hander*

*Paper position for left-hander*

## Why is a good posture important?

Developing a good posture is as important as developing a good pencil grip. Over the years children spend a great deal of time writing, and sitting in an awkward position can cause headaches, fatigue and pain in the shoulder, arm or hand. It can also slow down a child's writing. Children will be able to sustain writing for longer if they become used to sitting comfortably.

- Ensure that they have a good pencil grip – use commercial pencil grips only if other methods have failed.
- Check that tables are large enough so that the children aren't jostling each other's arms.
- Check the height of tables and chairs so children can sit comfortably, with their feet flat on the floor. Their legs should be free and not come into contact with the underside of the desk top. They should be able to sit up at the table without having to lean over it or stretch to reach it.
- The lighting should be good, so that the children can see what they have written.
- Children should have a direct view of the teacher/board
- Children should use their non-writing hand to steady the paper and bear some body-weight.
- The paper should be tilted slightly.
- Provide a slanting board for those who need it ( a partially filled A4 file is a useful shape).

*An example of good posture*

## Should I use formal worksheets to teach handwriting?

Not to begin with. While children are experimenting with shapes and letter forms, fluency of movement is most important. Size and neatness do not matter at this stage. Children enjoy experimenting with making patterns in sand or salt, using finger paints, marker pens, etc. and incorporating these into drawings, etc. Once children have had plenty of experience in drawing the letter shapes without constraints, they can then move onto using pencils and finer pens on smaller sheets of paper. For instance, you could cut out some green cabbage leaves for them to draw lots of caterpillars (**c**) on. The children could then cut a short slit up the stem, and with adult help, fold and staple a number of leaves together to form a cabbage. Likewise they could draw apples lying under a tree (**a**) or oranges growing in a tree (**o**). To start with, the children could trace over 'the apples' and you may want to put a mark at the point where the 'letter' begins. Then they can go on and do some more by themselves. This sort of handwriting 'worksheet' has motivational appeal and will help in the development of fine motor control.

## Why is a good pencil grip important?

If children are to develop a fluent and fast handwriting style, they must learn to hold a pencil with a grip that is relaxed but allows for efficient control of the pencil. If children grip a pencil too tightly, they won't develop a free-flowing movement and they will tire very quickly. Experts agree that children should be encouraged to hold the pencil between the thumb and forefinger with the pencil resting on the third finger. The thumb and forefinger should also be able to move slightly so that very fine movements required for writing are possible. Commercial pencil grips, or triangular pencils, can be used to encourage this pencil hold but their use must be monitored as they can be misapplied. Care should be taken that children do not grip the pencil too tightly as this produces tenseness in the arm and shoulder and also increases pressure on the paper.

## Left-handed children

At least 10 per cent of the population is left-handed – a slightly higher proportion of males. There is no need for left-handed children to be disadvantaged when writing, if a few simple strategies are employed:

- Model letter formation, sky writing, etc. specifically for left-handed children, with your left hand.
- Make sure that left-handed children sit on the left of right-handed children, otherwise their writing arms will clash.
- Put a mark at the left side of the page to indicate where writing begins as some left-handed children mirror-write from the right.
- Left-handed children usually need to have the paper slightly to the left of centre of their body and should be encouraged to tilt their work clockwise so they can see what they have written.
- Experiment with seat height – some left-handed children may need a higher seat to view their work clearly and to prevent the elbow locking into their side as they work across the paper.
- To avoid smudging their work:
  - left-handed children should be encouraged to position their fingers about 1.5 cm away from the end of their writing implement;
  - the pencil should sit in the 'V' between thumb and forefinger, sitting parallel to the thumb;
  - the wrist should be straight.
- Writing from left to right is more difficult for left-handed children. They should, therefore, be given more attention in the classroom to ensure that they do not learn bad habits of position, posture and pen hold which will deter a fast, fluent and legible hand.

## Ascenders and descenders

Getting the movement of the letter right is one aspect of securing good handwriting. Establishing the relationship between the position of the letters is another. Lined paper (or the fine squared paper used on the continent) is essential. Show the children that the 'body' of the descenders (g, j, p, q, y), the bits which sit on the line, are the same height as the x letter (a, c, e, i, m, n, o, r, s, u, v, w, x, z). In most styles, the letter t is shorter than the other ascenders b, d, h, k, l. The letter f is distinguished by the variety of ways it is written.

## When should I introduce joined up writing?

As soon as possible once children are secure in the movements of each letter.

Words such as at, am, it, in, up make good starting points. Some rimes work well: pin, win, tin, bin, din, etc. Rimes containing the vowels a and o are harder to join into from the base because the pencil has to travel up and round to the starting point of the letter, eg *cat*, *dog*, and should be avoided at the beginning. In *Progression in phonics*, digraphs – where two letters stand for one sound – are introduced from step 3. If you introduce each digraph as one joined unit, that reinforces phonics and handwriting, using multi-sensory channels to reinforce both. As soon as possible, you can start encouraging the use of joined writing for practising some of the high frequency words too, to help to reinforce the fact that these words need to be remembered as wholes, eg *the, little, was, one*.

Most letters join with diagonal lines, eg *man, child*. When children start joining into n and m, there is a tendency to go into the base of the letter rather than using a diagonal join to the top of the letter. Draw children's attention to the letters which join from the top: o, v, w. The actual shape of the letter e depends upon whether the preceding letter finishes at the top of the x height or the bottom. For instance, when e follows d, it will simply be a loop; when it follows f, it is more likely to have the traditional e shape. Joining all letters has been shown to inhibit fluency. Many styles do not join after letters that finish to the left (s, b, j, g, y). Refer to the Year 2 handwriting objectives in the National Literacy Strategy *Framework for teaching*: the four basic joins.

## How does handwriting practice link into emergent/developmental writing?

Ideally, children need to be supervised when they are practising handwriting until letter formation is secure – bad habits reinforced in the Foundation Stage are difficult to eradicate later on. Children who have experienced the multi-sensory approach to learning letter shapes are less likely to develop bad handwriting habits. The holistic approach to learning handwriting and phonics together is an ideal basis for emergent writing because children become used to thinking about letter shapes and sounds together. As children begin to join letters to write digraphs and some high frequency words, their writing and spelling will become increasingly accurate.

## Should I be teaching handwriting during the Literacy Hour, or at other times?

Both! The word level part of the Literacy Hour, which focuses on phonics, is an ideal channel for reinforcing the movement of letter shapes while you work on their sounds. The children can use skywriting or marker pens on dry-wipe boards (ideally with wide lines drawn on them) to reinforce the letter shape as they say the sounds and do the activities recommended in *Progression in phonics*. Occasionally, in shared writing, demonstrate how knowledge of letter shapes and sounds is used when writing words and sentences. Choose sentences that include the target sounds/letters and talk about the hand movements for letter formation as you write the letters.

But the teaching of letters will occur outside the Literacy Hour. Even when the letters are learned, children should be allowed a few minutes each day to practise, simply concentrating on developing accuracy, fluency and speed without the distraction of spelling and composing text. As for all motor skills, long practice sessions spaced apart are much less productive than short and frequent sessions. Handwriting practice should be 'little and often', a few minutes at a time to practise a particular set of letters.

## Handwriting policies

A handwriting policy should include information about:
- what the school's specific aims and objectives for handwriting are;
- how the curricula for the Foundation Stage and National Curriculum are to be covered with direct reference to the objectives in the National Literacy Strategy *Framework for teaching*;
- how letters are to be formed and the agreed 'patter' to accompany the movement (ideally there should be a sheet showing both individual letter formation and which letters are joined and how);
- how the school's preferred style of handwriting is to be shared with parents;
- the extent to which children are encouraged to develop individual writing styles;
- provision for left-handed children;
- how handwriting is to be taught throughout the school, including the Foundation Stage;
- recommended writing materials and implements, eg paper sizes, line spacings, when children are expected to write with pens;
- provision for children with special educational needs;
- advice on classroom management, eg balance of whole class, group and individual instruction; furniture layout;
- provision for children who join the school in Year 1 or Year 2 with a different, but equally acceptable style of writing.

**Alphabet showing starting point and direction of each letter**

## Developing spelling

In order to be an efficient speller, a child needs to:

- be able to segment words into component phonemes;
- know which letters represent the phonemes in words;
- be able to distinguish visually between words which are 'legitimately' spelled, eg wait, wate;
- know the meanings of homophones, eg been and bean, so that the correct spelling is used;
- recall, eg by mental image, by memorising order of letters, 'tricky' words;
- know spelling conventions, eg relating to doubling letters;
- look for similarities in the spellings of words which are etymologically related, eg sign, signal.

## Emergent writing

Children's very early writing is 'mark-making with intent'. They imitate those whom they see writing by reproducing squiggly lines or letter- and number-like shapes. They invest these marks with meaning so, although lacking a regular code which can be comprehended, the marks can legitimately be described as writing. We encourage very young children's 'emergent' writing because discovering that print carries meaning is a giant stride towards literacy.

However, simultaneously, children are becoming increasingly:

- able to discriminate the sounds around them (early phonics – *see below*), and they also
- take an interest in the welter of print which surrounds them (early graphics – *see below*).

### Early phonics

- Most children are very sensitive to differences in sounds. For instance, a child can pick out the sound of his sister's motor bike from that of her friend's, or the bark of one neighbour's dog from another.
- They usually recognise the full complement of phonemes within the language and most young children are able to pronounce them all. In many of their games they use isolated phonemes to represent sounds, eg in a game of Thomas the Tank, the ch-ch-ch-sh-sh-sh of the steam train slowing down; pneumatic drills are often represented by d-d-d-d-d.
- Rhymes are children's first experience of replacing the phoneme at the beginning of a word, eg muddle, puddle.
- Children also enjoy focusing on the initial phoneme in words in other ways such as in alliterative jingles and games.

*Progression in phonics* steps 1 and 2 suggest lots of ideas for developing children's natural propensity for distinguishing sounds in the environment and phonemes in words.

### Early graphics

- Most children are surrounded by the 26 letters which make up the English alphabet – on signs, posters, food packaging, computer keyboard, labels and so on.
- Children pick out what is significant to them, particularly when their attention is drawn to it, eg their own name, others' names and certain prominent labels.
- Children will put a lot of effort into reproducing their own names and will voluntarily trace around the letters on the street signs on housing estates, which are just at their height, often saying the name in a protracted manner as they do it.
- Children will give names to letters in any way suggested by an adult – letter name, letter sound or suggestive character, eg Sammy Snake.
- Children can play games to facilitate the movements underpinning handwriting.

Section 3 on page 156, 'Developing handwriting' answers a number of questions relating to the teaching of handwriting.

The capacity of children to move on from expressing meaning through squiggly lines or letter- and number-like shapes is considerable and spelling words which have a closer relationship to the norm gives them enormous satisfaction. Children's earliest attempts at spelling need not be hindered by a lack of pencil control. Magnetic letters make an excellent temporary alternative; another alternative, the computer, is less temporary.

## Early spelling

There are two ways in which young children spell:

- by segmenting a word into its constituent phonemes
- by visually recalling the letters in a word.

### SEGMENTING A WORD INTO ITS CONSTITUENT PHONEMES

Early phonics and early graphics combine to produce a eureka moment when children discover that there is a relationship between the *phoneme* they hear at the beginning of a word and the *letter* they see at the beginning of the word. Once this concept is established, children quickly learn to identify the phoneme at the end of words and then the medial vowel. This is clearly described in steps in *Progression in phonics*, pages 14 and 15; the rest of the book provides activities to enable children to move from step to step. Daily sessions of phonics adding up to at least 15 minutes are needed to ensure that children acquire the phonemic skills for spelling and reading. Children who receive the rich and varied experience described in this book and *Progression in phonics* can spell words containing adjacent consonants, eg stand, and make a good approximation of words containing vowel digraphs, eg scream, screem, screme, by the end of the Reception year.

### APPLYING SKILLS OF SEGMENTATION TO THE PROCESS OF WRITING

The games in *Progression in phonics* are fun and children quickly acquire segmentation skills. For the children, the game is an end in itself, but there is no intrinsic merit in being able to match two objects which end in the same phoneme as in Jump in the hoop – step 3. Unless this ability is applied to spelling words, the activity is meaningless. You could use some of the phonics time to consolidate the work at step 3 by writing a sentence on the board with the children telling you what letters to write at the beginning and ends of each word. (Very able children in the class will probably furnish you with the vowels as well.) The sentence you construct for this purpose should include some regular CVC words, eg then, and some words where giving the beginning and end phonemes would be an acceptable approximation, eg stand. This encourages children to realise that they can have a stab at any word they wish to write. You would, of course, fill in the extra letters, with a brief explanation.

In shared writing time, the main focus will be on composition of ideas into sentences, but occasionally point out how you have spelled a word or ask the children to contribute to a spelling. In their independent writing, expect to see words written in accordance with children's accruing knowledge.

- For instance, at *Progression in phonics* step 2 expect children to represent the correct letter for the phoneme in initial position in a word, so long as they know the letter.
- Similarly, at step 3, expect them to represent the initial and final phonemes, again subject to their letter knowledge.
- At step 4, expect children to write CVC words and also to make a reasonable representation of other words: 'it macs me laf wen he frituns evre wun' (it makes me laugh when he frightens everyone).
- At step 5, children will be hearing both consonants in a cluster. However, most children can segment those at the beginnings of words, eg fl–, br–, earlier than those at the end, eg –nt, –lp.

- At step 6, children know one representation for each long vowel phoneme so their writing should show most phonemes represented by letters, although the di/trigraph may be inaccurate.
- Step 7 teaches the full range of digraphs and trigraphs and children begin to make correct choices on the basis of frequency of use of the di/trigraph in the language or visual recognition.

## VISUALLY RECALLING THE LETTERS IN A WORD

Children's names and very common words will be learned in this manner. Many short, frequently occurring, phonemically irregular (tricky) words must also be learned like this, eg one, they, was. Module 2 Unit 3 of the NLS *Distance Learning Materials* (1998), pages 7–10, contains tips for teaching these words. These materials indicate which common words must be learned visually, and which may be attempted phonemically. Use your knowledge of phonics (see the *Progression in phonics* CD-ROM) to ascertain which other words you will need to teach children and which they should be able to figure out using phoneme–grapheme correspondence.

## DECIDING WHICH STRATEGY FOR EACH WORD

Learning letters and using them to 'have a go' at the spellings of words gives greater scope to most children to write than learning to write whole words because learning to write whole words takes a long time. However, children do and should learn to write whole words. In effect, when writing, the child should ask himself, 'Do I know how to spell this word?' If, having written the initial letter (using the phonemic approach) the rest of the word does not suggest itself, the child should complete the word using the phonemic strategy. It's only when you know how to spell a word that you know whether it is phonemically regular or irregular (tricky). Children need to build up a body of correctly spelled 'tricky' words which they can spell correctly automatically; they need to know which words they can spell automatically.

## SPELLING PRACTICE

Spelling must become automatic. Children should be given the opportunity to practise spelling words. However, we all know children who can spell words correctly when they are concentrating on single words and don't have to worry about any other aspect of writing. We can support children's spelling by reducing the number of things they have to think about when they write. This scaffolding needs to be gradually removed so that children will spell words correctly in their independent writing. So, in spelling practice with each block of new spellings we can ask them to write words, later short and longer sentences. Finally, we can also ask them to compose a sentence on a subject already discussed in full. Given this attention, we should expect to see these words correctly spelled in their independent writing.

## Linking handwriting, phonics and spelling practice

### SEGMENTING AND BLENDING, LINKING TO HANDWRITING

- Demonstrate CVC word-building, using known phonemes. The children try for themselves on individual lined dry-wipe boards.
- Pronounce CVC word. The children write it on their dry-wipe boards.

As children's phonic knowledge develops, the same technique can be used for CCVC words, etc., and for building CVC words using vowel digraphs.

### SPELLING IRREGULAR KEY WORDS, LINKING TO HANDWRITING

- Demonstrate how to write a simple key word, eg the, was, said, as a joined unit. This reinforces the importance of treating these words as 'wholes'.
- The children try for themselves, first sky writing, then on individual dry-wipe boards.

● Say one or two of the words previously practised aloud. The children write it/them on their dry-wipe boards as joined units.

### WRITING SENTENCES (CONCENTRATING ON SOUND–SYMBOL ASSOCIATIONS)
● Write a short sentence featuring key phonemes/sight words.
● The children try the same or a similar sentence on individual dry-wipe boards.
● Dictate a simple short sentence. The children write it on their dry-wipe boards.

### MAKING THE LINK TO WRITING FOR MEANING
● Model handwriting, making occasional links to phonics and spelling, as part of shared writing.
● In supported composition and independent writing, the teacher reminds the children to use their knowledge of phonics and related handwriting skills to transcribe their own words and sentences.

## Three games to practise spelling (and handwriting)

### Word-spell
● Have a set of eight word cards. These could be a set of 'tricky' words the children have recently learned or they could be a set of words which the children can write by segmenting.
● Place them in a pile face down.
● Give the children dry-wipe boards, one between two.
● Ask a child to be the teacher and to turn over the top card and read out the word.
● One child in each pair writes the word and shows it to his or her partner.
● The partner inspects the word and either agrees the spelling or suggests an amendment.
● The two children either agree the suggested change or write two versions on the board.
● The 'teacher' child shows the word to the class and all the children check that they have written correctly.
● The children discuss the 'tricky' bit of the word; the teacher makes a note, if necessary of the errors being made and which children are having difficulty.
● The 'teacher' child chooses another child to be the teacher.
● The alternative child in each pair does the writing next.

### Sentence-spell
Modify the procedure for 'Word-spell' using, first short and then longer sentences. The sentences should include a mixture of well-known words and some recently learned ones. For longer sentences, it may be more appropriate for all the children to write the sentence on notepads and compare with a partner.

### Sentence-make
Discuss the subject matter of the sentence which contains the spellings you wish to practise. Let the children compose the actual sentence themselves. They now have to consider the composition, the spelling, the handwriting and the punctuation.

## Spelling conventions
By Year 2, children need to start assimilating some of the spelling conventions into their writing. Objectives for teaching these are in the NLS *Framework for teaching*.